SIGN TO
STORY

SIGN TO STORY

LET NOTHING HOLD YOU BACK FROM
LIVING THE STORY OF YOUR LIFE

CHRISTOPHER DAVID SMITH

Charleston, SC
www.PalmettoPublishing.com

Sign to Story

First Edition.

Paperback ISBN: 978-1-64990-769-1

This book is dedicated to my wife, Kristy, who loves me completely despite my rough edges; to my son, Jackson, who always reminds me to live this life without fear; and to my daughter, Mollie, who continues to teach me the power of moments. Finally, it is dedicated to every person who forsakes comfort or convenience, position or prosperity, and tradition or trial to live their story and follow Jesus.

TABLE OF CONTENTS

INTRODUCTION

I'll never forget that Wednesday. I was leaving a shopping area to head to church and pulled up to a stop sign. I looked out my window and saw him. He was around my age. He had a rough beard coming in and worn, slightly dirty clothes. Now, I have seen homeless people before on the road. My wife interned in college at a homeless shelter and knew the homeless population well. We have spoken numerous times about how many people view homelessness as a way of life. There are addicts, those that enjoy the lifestyle, those that get caught in a cycle, and those who truly have had a season of tough luck. It's not my place to judge, but knowing exactly what to do to help in the moment is somewhat difficult.

I've handed out money before, but that's usually not my go-to method. I have bought food for a few homeless people in our community, given away some gift cards, and tried to keep some Bibles or Christian workbooks close if I feel led to share those as well. One summer, our kids at church made baggies to hand out with bottled water, snack crackers, hand sanitizer, a small gospel track, and a gift card. One cold day, I even felt compelled to give away my beloved Chicago Cubs blanket that I had in my trunk. Boy did I feel like that was a huge sacrifice! I try to do my part. If I can get out of my own way, I like to be like Jesus.

This time was different. All the standard pieces were in place. He looked homeless. He was unkept. He did not appear to have showered recently, and certainly looked a little rough for wear. He had his cardboard sign that was simple enough. In fact, it was the simplicity that caught my attention. His sign was not advertising that he would work for food. It didn't tell me that he had recently lost his job or had a family of five waiting at home. It was the simplest sign I had ever encountered. It said two words: "NEED HELP".

Those two words spoke deep into my soul. All of a sudden, I was transported to the throne room of God, and I was standing before Him, God Almighty, with the same two words on my feeble cardboard sign. I did not know why those words hit me like never before, but I realized we all must face the reality that we must stand before God each day and simply declare, "Need Help".

The realization was twofold. It was more than just my own incomplete and desperate state, but the hard truth that we allow ourselves to be judged by one or two words that define us for the world to observe.

We are defined by our past—Failure, Divorced, Liar, Abused, Ashamed, Addict, Doubter, Fraud, Unloved, Has-Been, or Never-Was.

We are defined by our current state. Most jobs can be summed up in one word—Nurse, Lawyer, Teacher, Janitor, Cashier, Waitress, Salesman, Driver.

Our relationships are also usually defined in one word—Married, Separated, Single, Friend, Husband, Wife, Sister, Brother, Dad, Mom.

Our own personalities find one word will often fit them as well—Funny, Sad, Bitter, Happy, Friendly, Depressed, Lonely, Positive, Eccentric.

Our attempts to balance all that life throws at us usually leaves us with one-word definitions too—Anxious, Tired, Lost, Fearful, Struggling, Juggling, Failing.

We continue to be defined by our future state, or at least what we think our future will hold—Happiness, Uncertainty, Change, Retirement, Loneliness, Loss.

Why do we let ourselves be defined so easily? Perhaps, because it is true. Like the man holding his sign, this was his reality. He did truly "Need Help." Yet, I would challenge all of us that we accept these signs and words with too much ease. Many of us have come to wear our signs as badges of honor. We almost take a sense of pride in being tired, struggling, anxious, or juggling. There's a reason the guys in the circus who are good at juggling are called clowns! It's great for entertainment, but it doesn't get you anywhere. You find yourselves juggling the same things over and over, and are caught in a mind-numbing and dangerous loop. Stop!

If Jesus promised "life to the full," then why do we accept anything less? CS Lewis said it best,

x

It would seem that Our Lord finds our desires not too strong, but too weak. We are half-hearted creatures, fooling about with drink and sex and ambition when infinite joy is offered us, like an ignorant child who wants to go on making mud pies in a slum because he cannot imagine what is meant by the offer of a holiday at the sea. We are far too easily pleased.

God has BIG plans for you. They are bigger than you can even imagine. But in order for us to find them, we have to do a few things with purpose. We must look deep. We must look deeper than our own thoughts and self-reflection. We must look into the very depths of creation. My momma always told me, "God didn't make any junk." And she was right! We were all created for a purpose and for a reason. There is a God-written story inside us all. We must commit to finding this purpose and living our stories. I've learned that even in the pursuit of this purpose, we can uncover a lot about what we should be doing every single day and in every single moment.

We must redefine our sign. We should never be able to be described in such few words. The next time someone asks you what you do for a living, don't give them a one-word response! Blow their minds with a statement that tells more about who you are and why you were created. Tell them that you are a passionate lover of life who tries to place joy and hope in the lives of others. Share with them that you strive to be the best mother or father or husband or wife or brother or sister you can possibly be on a daily basis and that Westley's motto in *The Princess Bride* is exactly right. In twenty years of marriage, I wish I would have always responded to every single one of my wife's requests, "As you wish!" I have a wonderful relationship with her, but this would have only made it better. Tell them what your dreams are, and what you are currently doing and pursing to reach those dreams. Share with them about the victories God has brought you through, and where you feel like He is leading you now.

Finally, we need to lose the sign. You are more than a sign. You are much greater than any word! You are charged with changing your "sign" into a "story." Never allow people to look at you the same way again. Live your life in such a way that it is a constant story. I love Bob Goff. The main reason is that he keeps the purpose of life so simple! He loves people. He loves every single one of them. He doesn't discriminate. He just loves anyone God places in his path. A great thing happens when you do this each day. These experiences make the best stories, and Bob tells the best stories. Jesus did the same thing. He loved everyone. He told some incredible stories too. It's high time we change our "sign" into a "story."

In the three sections that follow, I want you to go on a journey with me. I'm writing this as I'm trying to live out my story as well. I certainly don't have it figured out, but I'm willing to pursue it with all I have in me. I want to desperately seek out why God created me, and live this life to the fullest. I want to share stories with everyone I meet about what God is doing in me and through me. I want my life to be a story that's worth being told.

Take a breath. Throw definitions out the window. Gather up your few belongings and quit standing still. Fold up your cardboard sign. Life is calling. Jesus is calling. Let's write your story together.

Section 1

SEEING THE REAL ME BEHIND MY SIGNS

I have a dimple. In my opinion, it's what defines my face. I also shave my head. Alright, truthfully and since we are being real, I'm pretty much bald. Shaving my head is what I do to make me look and sound cool. I'm not that tall. In Asian countries, I would be declared as having "average height," but here in America, I'm short. I've got a stocky frame which is great for a lot of things, except for buying nice clothes. For some reason, no one likes to make dress shirts and pants for someone my build. And don't even get me (or my wife especially) started on jeans.

How would you describe yourself? If you are being honest, what characteristics do you allow the world to see? Which ones do you work quite hard to hide? You must be willing to see yourself clearly. You may feel the world has already defined you, but the time has come to define yourself on the basis of how and why you were created.

DO ME A FAVOR. LOOK IN THE MIRROR? WRITE DOWN WHAT YOU SEE. USE ONE- TO TWO-WORD STATEMENTS.

- _____
- _____
- _____
- _____
- _____
- _____
- _____

1

REALITY VS. CREATED SIGNS

My guess is that most of the words you used in the previous exercise carried a negative connotation. Many people will tell you to not listen to the "voice" inside your head about all these negative statements. What they forget many times is that it is rarely one voice that you hear. Sure, we hear our own voice, but we also hear the voices of those who have shared their opinions before today. Most of the time, we don't remember the compliments; it's the criticisms that take hold. All of these voices carry various amounts of weight. Before long, we are walking around carrying hundreds or thousands of pounds of weight that God never intended for us to shoulder. Is it any wonder that we look and feel tired? These are the signs we created to define our own image and to match our own thoughts.

Jesus has something to say about all those voices and all these burdens. He tells us to take on His yoke because it is easy and His burden is light (Matthew 11:30). He also tells us to listen to one voice – His (John 10:27). The reason His yoke is easy and His burden is light is because it involves only listening to ONE voice. Jesus tells us we are His treasure, and are His masterpiece (Ephesians 2:10). He continually reminds us that we are His most prized possession and that He literally gave His life for each one of us (John 15:13)!

The next time you look in the mirror, hear His truth. Know that those wrinkles mean you have lived with purpose. Those scars show the experiences you have come through. The slightly gray hair signifies wisdom you can pass on to others. The extra weight represents the time you have spent with your kids rather than in the gym. It may be the choices you made to have ice cream more often with your family too.

WHAT DOES JESUS SAY ABOUT YOU?

You are precious in my eyes, and honored, and I love you – *Isaiah 43:4*

I am fearfully and wonderfully made. – *Psalm 139:14*

We are His workmanship, created in Christ Jesus for good works, which God prepared beforehand, that we should walk in them. – *Ephesians 2:10*

He cares for you. – *1 Peter 5:7*

If anyone is in Christ, he is a new creation. – *2 Corinthians 5:17*

If God is for us, who can be against us? – *Romans 8:31*

NOTHING will be able to separate us from the love of God in Christ Jesus our Lord. – *Romans 8:39*

See what kind of love the Father has given to us, that we should be called children of God; and so we are. – *1 John 3:1*

What is Jesus speaking to you right now? What would He say to you if He looked at you?

Look in the mirror again. This time, I want to challenge you to hear a different voice. I want you to only think about the positive statements others have made about you. Remember the time someone complimented your smile, your wit, your hair, your laugh, or your eyes? Think about a time someone told you that you did an amazing job. What characteristics did they notice about you?

We all have a choice each morning when we wake up and look in the mirror. I'm reminded of the Evil Queen from the movie *Snow White*. She waltzes over to the magic mirror every day and asks, "Mirror, Mirror, on the wall, who's the fairest of them all?" As a young child I was mesmerized. It was not for a good reason. Even in the Disney version, she is super scary! When I was a kid, I actually remember thinking that this lady was the farthest thing from a "fair" lady as you could get.

Then, we went to see Snow White at Disney World last year. I was forty years old. We had dinner with Snow White and some of the dwarves, and had a wonderful family meal. The Evil Queen stood over near the exit, and you could get your picture taken with her when you left. She never broke character. I watched her almost the whole time. She glared at everyone. She never smiled. Her comments were cold and sometimes harsh. But, she was really pretty. If I'm being honest and real (and we are), she was a very attractive lady. I couldn't help but think if she would have just been content with her looks and her life, it would have turned out a lot better for her. She had some attractive qualities but couldn't see them, at least not enough to be content. So instead of embracing her beauty that was on the outside and working on the inside, she turned into an ugly, old witch and died. I wonder how different her story would have been if she had worried a little less about another's beauty, and just embraced her own.

Competition is real. I see it every day with my wife, my daughter, my coworkers and colleagues, and even with my son. It comes in many different shapes and options and apps on the phone. How many days do you look at your phone before you even look in the mirror? What are you comparing yourself to when you look in either? You have already set yourself up and started telling yourself the same lies—I'll never have hair like so and so. (I personally put this to bed a long time ago and have actually enjoyed being bald.) I wish my figure or muscles looked like theirs. I've cut back on sugar and soft drinks but I can't lose this extra weight around my midsection and have a waist like...

We stand in front of the mirror and hold our sign so big and tight that we don't actually see ourselves. We fail to see what makes us special and unique!

Our competition mindset is as productive as chasing the wind. It is there and it is real, but it is unattainable. Most importantly, it will never get you what you really want. Years from now, when you look back on what you pursued, will you be proud of where you spent your time, your focus, and your energy? There's a great video from Kyle Martin, a graduating senior, who decided he wanted to be valedictorian of his high school class. He stayed focused, worked hard, and achieved his goal. In his speech to his fellow seniors, he reminded them of the sixteenth second. He shared about when they announced he was the valedictorian, the top, the best in his class—it felt great. This award was such an accomplishment. It was a wonderful feeling, which lasted for fifteen seconds. In the sixteenth second, Kyle realized that while it felt great and was a big accomplishment, it had cost him a lot to get to that point. He missed out on some other great opportunities in his pursuit of this goal and dream. He was vulnerable enough to admit his struggle and share his story. He was pursuing something good, but potentially at the cost of missing out on something great.

Our pursuit of this idea of what we could be or should be when we look at others probably won't even last ten seconds. We will convince ourselves we need to immediately start doing something else to change our look, our body, our influence. Perhaps, we will look back and realize this was not energy well-spent. I'm not saying you can't focus on change. All I am suggesting is that this focus should not be singular and take you away from your God-given purpose.

You know what is attractive? Confidence. I have a friend who is my height, small-framed, wears glasses, doesn't have straight teeth, and is missing that defined jaw line. Yet when he walks into a room, he owns it. He has a caring and genuine personality, and people gravitate towards him. I have studied him and finally figured it out. It is his confidence. It is not arrogance. There is a big difference between the two. He is completely comfortable just being him. He loves God and knows God loves him. I believe this helps tremendously. He has a passion for his job, his relationships, and his life. He does not try to be the best at everything; he simply gives his best. He is not the greatest singer, but is a dynamic worship leader. He isn't the best guitar player or drummer, but he plays any instrument with passion and purpose. All this combines to form a confident and attractive person. Attractive just means "appealing to look at." It doesn't mean that you have all the indistinguishing qualities. It also can mean "inducing someone to accept what is being offered." When you walk in the confidence that God made you special and just the way you are, you are telling others to accept what you bring and what you are offering. That's it. Why would you not offer the world exactly what God made you to be?

You can see yourself in light of the negative comments, the celebrity Instagram posts, your neighbor next door, and your friend from high school, or you can listen to the voice of God. You can remind yourself that you were created in the image of a glorious God and Creator, and that you are wonderfully made. Or, you can analyze the new wrinkle or the bags under your eyes. You know, the same ones your other friend covers up with makeup.

Drop the sign! Quit standing there holding it! It's time to embrace what makes you, you!

WRITE DOWN THE QUALITIES YOU WILL "OWN." LOOK
DEEPLY AT WHO GOD CREATED YOU TO BE AND HOW
HE DESIGNED YOU! DON'T THINK ABOUT ANYTHING
ELSE THAN WHAT GOD GAVE YOU. WRITE DOWN
YOUR "ATTRACTIVE OR PLEASING QUALITIES."

- _____
- _____
- _____
- _____
- _____
- _____
- _____

Remember them. Own them. Promise yourself that you will focus on these positive affirmations, and you will move forward without holding up the same old, negative sign.

We all need a reality check. This is part of the problem, but you and I both know it is not the core issue. The greatest test we face is not what lies on the outside, but on the inside. The pressure is intense. It's the thought of missing out. It is the fear of less. It's the hope of more. It's the wonder if this is all life has to offer, and the settling for something far too small.

Bebo Norman, a great Christian singer and songwriter, calls it "the ache." He says it is the reminder that we are not at home yet in Heaven where all will be made perfect. It is what tugs inside of us all the time in this imperfect world. There is the dream and the hope and the pursuit of something greater, continually combating the reality of a fallen world where life does not happen like we wish. All I know on this side of heaven, God has a grand story for you to live that never involves settling for anything less than His best!

2

TRUE FREEDOM VS. COLLECTED SIGNS

I don't know exactly where you are at in this life, but I bet it's not where you thought it would be in this moment. That's actually a really good thing. We hold our signs as a part of our "collection." The signs are familiar. They provide a sense of comfort and maybe even relief because they are how we are known. The worst thing we can do with our signs is to become super comfortable. When we embrace our signs, it becomes far too easy to live a life that forgets our gifts and strengths or takes them for granted. These signs exist as a constant temptation to throw aside what God created us to do in this life.

I had a good friend growing up who collected Star Wars items, and they were awesome! He had them set up on small shelf-like slats in between the 2x4 studs in his unfinished basement. He had action figures, spaceships, and all the rarest collectibles. He even had a full-size Darth Vader helmet! Everything was unopened. If you have collected anything, you know it is worth more if it is in the original packaging. The Star Wars items sat on shelves and starred at me. It was really neat until I realized they weren't good for anything but looking at and admiring. They were designed to be toys. Toys are supposed to be played with and enjoyed. Life is supposed to be lived to the fullest.

Your life is not designed to be comfortable, simple, easy, and uneventful. Your life may look nice, orderly, and complete sitting on a shelf for others to admire. Just like collected toys, your life is missing its purpose if this is your goal. If you are proud that you can hold up all the signs you have collected thus far in life that say words like, "comfortable," "successful," or "has it all together," you are lying to yourself and the world. It is a false sign and a charade. It will not last. The cracks will begin to shine through. No one has it all together, and our definitions of success and comfort are way off base in our world today. These items or signs that we collect are not who we really are, and they cannot be how we are known. We are so much more than these signs. Like the unopened toys, your signs may capture a glimpse of who you are, but it is far from what you were created to be as you were designed for much greater things.

ANSWER THE FOLLOWING QUESTIONS FOR REFLECTION USING A SCALE OF 1-10.

I am where I want to be with...

my relationships: 1 2 3 4 5 6 7 8 9 10

my spouse: 1 2 3 4 5 6 7 8 9 10

my kids: 1 2 3 4 5 6 7 8 9 10

my friends: 1 2 3 4 5 6 7 8 9 10

my job: 1 2 3 4 5 6 7 8 9 10

serving others: 1 2 3 4 5 6 7 8 9 10

using the gifts God has given to me: 1 2 3 4 5 6 7 8 9 10

I love a great quote I once heard that says, "The two most important dates in your life are the day you were born and the day you find out why." Have you discovered why you were created? I don't know exactly where you are at in this life, but I pray you believe there is more to come and better things waiting. I pray you know how much God loves you and how He created you in His own image. I pray you realize that we live in a sinful and broken world, and that you (and I) are a part of that problem. There is plenty of blame to go around. We are all in this together.

Sin is anything you place in front of God or that goes against the nature and qualities of God. There are big sins and small sins. There are sins other people know about, and sins we keep to ourselves. Sins often become a part of our sign collection. We accept these sins and compare them against other people and other sins. We justify them, and either accept them or lie to ourselves they are not really sins in the first place. The longer we hold onto them, the more they begin to shape our identities and pave our journeys.

Sin destroys. It destroys relationships. It destroys hearts. It tears at the very fabric of life which we were created to embrace. Sin induces fear and hatred and feelings we do not need. It always leads us to a path that we didn't want to take in the first place or didn't even realize we were traveling. It is the great divider that leaves us stranded. The collected sign of any sin we continue carrying around is guaranteed to take us off course. This is where we start making our own signs, both created and collected ones.

We create and collect signs that say things like:

"It was his fault or her fault, not mine."

"Victim"

"I'm just being me!"

"I was cheated; I was wronged."

"Too scared to move"

"I hate you."

Yet God created an amazing way to get us back on course. God knew we would mess up because God is omniscient. He knows everything! At the beginning of time, God sent His Son on a journey. He told Jesus to start driving and look for someone who was very lost and way off course. Jesus started looking for all of us. God reminded Jesus that we would need a ride and some help. Jesus took off in His pristine white Cadillac with a mission to find us. Jesus pulled up beside us, every single one of us, and offered us the ride of a lifetime. Sometimes, we have refused. We have had all the excuses in the world.

"It's okay Jesus, I'm just going to keep walking on my own. I'll get where I'm going eventually."

"I could never get in your car. I'm too dirty. I wouldn't want to mess up your perfect white leather seats."

"I think you have me mistaken with someone else. I didn't call for a ride. I kind of like it out here and seem to be doing just fine."

"I'm going to keep walking, but I'll call later if I need you to swing back by."

"I almost didn't recognize you Jesus. My mom and my grandpa told me about you. It's nice to see you again, and I'll make sure I tell them you said hello."

Jesus drove for eternity to meet you. Are you really going to offer the Son of Man, the One who allowed everything in this world to be created through Him so that He could redeem it all, the One who suffered and died and bore your sins and mine and the sins of the world on an old rugged cross, some lame excuse?! He knows you intimately and completely. Jesus knows your collected sins and signs, and still loves you completely. He takes these sins and signs, and removes them as far as the east is from the west. He is the Way, the Truth, and the Life. He is love incarnate. He is God with us! Take the ride!

Get in the car. He could care less about how dirty you are, or where you were heading or that fact that you feel "fine." He is here to get you back on the right path and heading in the right direction. He has a plan that He created you for and wants to show you. He longs for you to use the gifts and talents He has given you to fulfill this plan. Sit down. Relax. Stay. He is going to show you things you can't even picture in your mind.

He wants to go on an epic journey with you. He wants to constantly remind you that the cross hanging up in His rearview mirror is Him! He loves you that much and will never stop loving you completely. He is here to guide you over every hill and through every valley. Let Him drive. He knows the way completely. Listen to His stories and enjoy His presence. Leave your old sign by the road, and let Him make you clean and whole.

If we are going to brace ourselves for what is real, we have to deal with the truth that we are dirty and broken and can never be whole apart from Jesus.

My buddy, Drew Hill, wrote an amazing book a few years ago called, *Alongside*. Drew and I used to serve in Young Life together when I had just finished college, and I was able to observe him firsthand. In his book, he talks about teenagers and how what they really want most is for someone to come alongside them in life. I watched Drew and other Young Life leaders continually come alongside kids and attend football games, school lunches, band competitions, and tennis matches, where they may have only been one of two people in the stands! "Alongside" is one of my new favorite words. It carries such weight and power because it truly means meeting people where they are and simply joining them in their journeys at a certain point in their stories.

Jesus set this example first. He came alongside a bunch of fishermen. He came alongside a tax collector. He came alongside a blind man, a demon-possessed man, a cripple, and a guy named Lazarus that had been dead for four days. Coming alongside someone is really only the beginning. You don't come alongside someone to leave them the way you found them! You come alongside because you are ready to walk with them on a new journey and remind them that they have a grand story to be lived. This is exactly what Jesus did for everyone He met. He challenged them, helped them, guided them to new possibilities, and showed them that there was more to the current life they were living. As we get back on course, commit to letting Jesus walk beside you every moment. Being real means that you can't do this alone.

3

YOUR GRAND STORY VS.
COMFORTABLE SIGNS

What signs have you become too comfortable with in your life and have added to your collection? In reality, we often just keep the same sign up because we've been carrying it around for so long that they have simply become a part of us. You may have taken a wrong turn, given up on a dream, or settled for less than the best that God has planned for you. We believed the lie that someone told us about what we were created to be or where this road of life might lead.

We have a unique opportunity every single day to keep carrying the same sign or to put it down and do something different. The sign is what keeps us stuck. It is the reminder of a great untruth that leads our lives. In many ways, it is the bondage that holds us back from being "more," and experiencing "more," and letting "more" of the things we love into our lives.

Allow me to be clear. "More" does not mean that all of us were created to change the world, at least not in the sense we often think. Who doesn't want more love, more hope, more laughter, more peace, more enjoyment, and more moments that we can look back on with pride and fulfillment. A great school leader that I heard present at a conference spoke of how we need to quit trying to be a world changer, who impacts many and, instead, focus on changing a world, one at a time. Embrace each opportunity God gives you to pour into the person standing in front of you. It is a singular focus. Look at the world around you and think about how you could help one person in a powerful manner. We all have the opportunity to do this for our children, our spouses, our coworkers, our friends, our neighbors, the orphan in a foreign country, or the homeless person on the side of the street.

Be honest with yourself. Which sign are you holding up each morning that keeps holding you back? Which sign or signs have you collected that are preventing you from being a changer of worlds? Is it "Tired," "Overwhelmed," "Parent," "Caregiver," "Stay-at-home Mom," or "Careerman," or "Careerwoman"? Are the signs you hold more of a waiting game like, "Hanging On," "Waiting for a new season," "Someday," "Maybe," "I couldn't," or "I shouldn't?"

There's a great story in the New Testament about a group of guys who were pretty comfortable with the signs they had collected. "Fisherman" was a prominent one. "Complacent" or "Settled" would have worked as well. "Tax Collector" was the one held tightly by Matthew. The day was very typical. They woke early to get their boats ready. They headed out on the sea before breakfast. They sat. They talked. They fished. It was the same as just about every day before it. Their dad was a fisherman, and it was just easy to settle into that lifestyle. Two words changed their lives forever. Jesus showed up and simply said, "Follow Me" (Matthew 4:19). They followed, and the rest is history. These twelve disciples all had their simple and settled signs ready to go each day. Jesus told them to forget the signs and focus on the adventure that lay ahead. Jesus promised them "more," and offered them a chance to be a changer of worlds.

Do you know that "fine" is my least favorite word in the English dictionary? I share this with just about everyone I meet. For twenty years, I have begged my wife to not mention that word if I ask her if she likes something or how she feels about anything. My least favorite sign would be the word, "Fine," as well. The problem is that we use this word a lot. I would argue that you have probably already said it at least five times today.

The problem with the word, "fine," is that it simply means okay. It is completely appropriate to use it to describe a Lean Cuisine meal you ate to satisfy your hunger, but not much else. It should certainly never be used to describe your life. Your life is meant for so much more. We wake up, judge ourselves, compare ourselves, question ourselves, doubt ourselves, and sometimes even drug ourselves (I'm counting caffeine and sugar in that statement as well), all so we can hold up our sign that says, "I'm fine." Do not ever settle for being comfortable with "fine."

It is okay to not be okay. We get comfortable convincing ourselves that we are okay and fine, and we have the signs to prove it. We should all be able to freely admit there are some days when it is a struggle. These days and these moments allow us to better analyze our lives. If we truly stop and think about the struggle, it is a good thing. Growth does not happen without a struggle. A baby chick must struggle to make its way out of the egg. It is in this struggle that the chick strengthens its lungs and muscles so it can survive. If I want to add muscles and strengthen my heart health and lungs, I must choose to work out, which can be very painful as well.

A few years ago, I made a commitment to myself and my family to get in better shape. I joined a workout group called F3. It stands for Fitness, Fellowship, and Faith. It should just be called "FT" for Fitness and Torture! Apparently, I joined the greatest group of fitness fanatics in the state of North Carolina. We run for miles, do hundreds of reps, and push our bodies in every possible way. It is always tough and often torturous. But, I am alive and in better health. It is a struggle, but it is worth it. Growth and change are never easy, but this is part of the growth process. This struggle and growth process are getting me closer to where I need to be in life.

We have to be willing to struggle. We must understand that we will fail. The deep truth lies in the fact that we all struggle and we all fail at times. This is not something most people are willing to be honest and vulnerable about, so we pretend it does not happen. I could never do the workouts that I do with my F3 group in my garage. Trust me; I've tried! There is something powerful about pushing each other, helping each other, and watching each other fail, only to come back stronger the next time. Growth is not pretty. It is the opposite of comfortable. Growth does not happen overnight, but it is real, and it is worth it. We must make this commitment, embrace the struggle, and learn from failure in order to truly grow.

IN WHAT AREAS OF YOUR LIFE ARE YOU WILLING
TO GROW AND EMBRACE THE STRUGGLE?

○ _____

○ _____

○ _____

○ _____

○ _____

○ _____

○ _____

Growth requires us to both see where we have been and where we are going. Every change and growth period in our lives must have a starting point. A pastor I once knew often said, "I'm not where I want to be, but praise God, I'm not where I was!" This is the same attitude we must embrace in the change. It is a struggle, and it is a process. The key is to keep moving forward. Only then, are we able to reflect on where we have been and where we are going. We are able to make adjustments and modify our course on this journey through life. An example we can probably all relate to is the "secret" art of losing weight. The only catch is, there is no "secret." We must consume less calories! If we really want to lose the weight, we have to eat fewer calories and burn more by working out longer and with more intensity. It is not a hard concept. My problem is that I don't like changing my eating habits and putting down the cookies, cakes, and confectionary delights!

I see the problem quite clearly. I know the steps I should take to accomplish my goals. I like to play the game, though, and see what I can get away with and how I can push the boundaries. It reminds me of a game that I played in high school called, "rolling yards." One of the greatest adventures we could take as a fourteen- to sixteen-year-old was to buy a bunch of cheap toilet paper, throw it in a trunk, pile as many people as we could into a car, and drive to the house of a classmate around midnight or later. We would park a couple of hundred yards away from our "friend's" house, each grab as much TP as we could carry, and sneak through the darkness. Once we arrived at our target, we hurled toilet paper as high as we could throw it into the tallest trees. It was like we were trying out for an Olympic sport! We laughed until we cried. Typically, it was about that time that a flood light would come on, and once again, we were in the Olympics. Only this time, we were in the 200-yard dash as we sprinted back to the car and took off.

I think back to why I did this when I was younger. What was the thrill, and did the reward really outweigh the risk? "Rolling" someone's yard was about pushing the boundary just enough and not getting in too much trouble. I put up the blinders around my boundaries. I set a boundary I could live with and then put blinders towards anything bad that may happen. I never thought someone would come out of the house with a gun. The police being called never crossed my mind. At least, not until it happened. Suddenly I was standing with my hands on the top of a police cruiser with a cop that, looking back, was probably just too upset that he was called at 1:20 a.m. for this foolishness. It got bad in a hurry. My "rolling yards" days went the way of the dodo bird. I had blinded myself to these consequences, all in the name of fun and excitement.

Too many of us use our signs as blinders as well. We hold our signs up at just the right angle where they don't allow us to see the full picture. I've done this plenty of times in my own life. The problem when you do not see the full picture though is there is usually something of danger close you do not see until it is too late. We do not want to think that the very signs we created and the signs we have become comfortable carrying would dare blind us from the world around us, but it has created a world where we often only see what we choose to see.

How many of you use the crop feature on your photos? Why do we do this to our pictures? We want to highlight the parts of our photos that we like best. We pull out what we deem as "good" and leave the rest behind like it was never there. I'm a huge Disney fan. One of the most iconic pictures you can take at Disney World is the picture in front of Cinderella Castle. The problem is no less than three hundred people are trying to capture the exact same moment every single second. People make a business of cropping castle photos to make it look like they were the only ones there. This is a façade and it is not real life! Those people were there; they were real, and they mattered. Maybe I'm being extreme, but we do this in our lives all the time. We hold up our created, comfortable, and collected signs so that we are front and center. We focus on what matters to us and what we want to see. In doing this, we often miss warning signs, other's reactions and feelings, and the reality of our actions and the consequences they hold.

Our son just recently received his driving permit. He is ready to conquer the world. His confidence is encouraging. It is also quite unsettling at times. While he is doing a good job and I want him to be confident with his driving, there are times he becomes too comfortable in the vehicle. The signs we collect can become quite comfortable in the driver's seats of our lives. The one thing I am desperately trying to teach him is that he must be aware of what is in front of him, beside him, and behind him. If he is merging lanes and doesn't see a car flying up fast, there is going to be a problem.

Life is like this often. There are lots of times when you feel everything is going well, and a problem flies up to overtake you out of nowhere. Other times, it is more of a slow fade. You may have been driving down the road for a while and just put it into autopilot. Everything appears to be going "fine." It isn't until you go to switch lanes that you realize another car has been in your blind spot the whole time.

Both situations have results that are destructive. I can argue all day long with the police officer that I just did not see the car. The injuries, medical bills, insurance claims, and damaged cars are not going to change over my argument. We argue with ourselves and our signs that we just did not see something coming. We did not know we were merging off our God-given paths, but we will still find ourselves in a mess. If we didn't crop out what we didn't like earlier, we could have most likely seen what was heading our way.

My weight gain didn't fly up from behind and hit me suddenly, so that I woke up one morning with an extra twenty-five pounds around my midsection. It was certainly a slow fade. I would argue that 98 percent of divorcees did not wake up one morning, have one single fight, and call it quits. The bitterness, unforgiveness, and loss of connection took place over time. Those feelings built and layered until they all spilled over and created a disastrous mess. The horrible, angry outburst may have hit suddenly, but it was just as real.

What have you been blinded to or have been blocking out? Are you aware of the emotional state of your family and friends? Do you just keep pushing on with your "I'm Too Busy," or "They Seemed Fine" collected signs to really notice? Is the sign of your job keeping you from seeing a better opportunity? Is the "They Need Me" sign keeping you tied to a relationship that you should have let go of a long time ago? Does your current emotional sign of "Depressed," "Frustrated," or "Angry" keep you from experiencing the joys the Lord is trying to direct you towards today?

PAUSE. ASK GOD TO SHOW AND REVEAL TO
YOU WHAT YOU HAVE BEEN BLIND TO AND HAVE
BLOCKED OUT. WRITE THEM DOWN.

- _____

- _____

- _____

- _____

- _____

- _____

- _____

I think back to those disciples Jesus called, and I wonder. Their world and their signs were "Fine." Life was probably going pretty well for most of those guys. Sure, Peter had some leadership qualities that could be used outside of the fishing boat, but at least he found others listened to his ideas and thoughts. James and Peter made quite the brother-fishing duo. Life could be mundane, and many days were like the ones before, but overall, they had a life to be proud of in their little town. There were moments though that surely, they both looked out over the sea and wondered if this job and routine offered enough excitement and used their God-given gifts and talents to the fullest. I wonder if they knew something greater was calling.

I can only imagine Matthew. He was making good money as a tax collector. He always took a little off the top for himself, but not as much as a few of the other guys he worked with each day. The dirty looks and mumbled comments did not sting like they once did when he started in this job. He came to expect them now. He had been invited to some of the more elite gatherings lately, and while it felt good to be around these wealthy and elite folks, they weren't much on having deep conversations. He often wondered aloud at night if there was a better balance to life and if money really did buy happiness. I wonder if a good job and money was enough and if he realized there were some things money could not buy.

Change is hard. In every instance of change, the companion is struggle. If change was easy then everyone would and could do it. The reality is we must do it! We must stop looking at ourselves in the mirror the same way, comparing ourselves to the same people, justifying why we are not satisfied, and being "fine" with our lives just like they are. We know there is more to this life, and we know we are being called to a different way of thinking and some different approaches. We must take that ride with Jesus behind the wheel and let Him lead. He won't let us be blindsided because He is already there. He will fight against the slow fade with His constant promises and reminders of love. Jesus is the very definition of change. The Bible says that if anyone is in Christ, with Jesus, they are a new creation (2 Corinthians 5:17). The old person, the old self, the old habits, and the old signs are gone. Jesus says He is making all things new (Revelation 21:5). That includes making you and I new, as well. It will feel like a struggle because it is fighting against our "human nature." You are more than your old self and your old ways and your old signs. Let's keep moving forward towards change and put the created and comfortable and collected signs to the side.

AN ADVENTURE OF A LIFETIME VS. OUR SIGNS AND OUR "FINE" LIFE

If we are not using our signs to tell ourselves a different story or to blind our view, we are using them as a "Badge of Honor" sign. These can be any signs we have collected, created, or become too comfortable carrying around with us. These signs allow us to justify many of our actions, and how we spend our time, and where we place our focus. These are the signs we have become far too comfortable with in our daily lives. I would do it, but I don't have the time, the resources, or the energy. I'm too busy taking my kids to club sports and four-times-a-week dance classes to even consider adding that to my schedule. This will make them more well-rounded, we tell ourselves. Sure, I could volunteer, but my job keeps me going at a good pace and I'm just too tired. My job requires a lot of me, and I must make my job the top priority.

The "I Don't Have Time" badge is the most used from my point of view.

"There is just no way I could fit that into my schedule. Even if I wanted to do that, I simply don't have the time."

Let's talk about time a little bit. Time is constant. Each day holds the same twenty-four hours. The seconds, the minutes, and hours always move at the same speed. We have already discussed that time does seem to fly and we can see the effects in the mirror. Time itself is not to blame. Time does not have it out for us and is not out to get us. Time does not make an agenda on how it can push us to the limit and stress us. Time is neutral.

Why do we blame time on a daily basis? I'm not Albert Einstein. I don't understand physics and relativity very well. I wish I could explain more about how time is relative, but I believe time became our enemy the moment sin entered the world.

Adam and Eve had it made. They spent their days exploring, discovering, and naming the different types of animals that existed in the garden (Genesis 2:9, 15). They laughed and talked and never argued. They were both the single most attractive man and woman in the entire universe. They never got sick and did not have a worry in the world. In the evenings, God would come walk with them and talk with them and tell them how special they were to Him. They had all the time they ever wanted and never rushed to do anything. One may say that time was on their side.

I would love to say that this never changed. But it did change, and it was bad. The devil wooed them and used their signs against them. He argued that they should be known as more than just "Best Gardeners," "Cutest Couple," and "God's Friends." The devil convinced them they should want signs that said, "Powerful," "All-Knowing," and "God's Equal." They bought the lie. They felt like they deserved more. They had God's best and the perfect relationship with Him, but for some reason, they wondered if it was enough. We still do the same today.

The "I Deserve" badge is the most destructive.

"Because I do this and because I do that, I deserve to be able to do what I want."

This sign gets people into deep trouble. Stop and think about places you do not want to end up and this sign is most likely at the center. Why do so many people carry deep credit card debt or end up in financial ruin? How does the perfect family end up with one spouse having a secret affair? How does the drug or alcohol addiction take hold? How does the world have so many needs, yet houses filled with so much stuff?

I try very hard not to judge people. Jesus said that I really can't see very well to judge them anyway. I've got my own issues and my own plank in my eye. I really don't know their circumstances and where the specks in their eyes come from or why they are there (Matthew 7:1-5). Just like the comparison struggle from the phone and mirror we discussed earlier, many of these signs we hold as a badge of honor start with something we see or think about someone else. There's no need to judge; we are all in a very similar situation.

We are a lot like Adam and Eve. We have been blessed beyond measure in so many ways, but we deeply feel we deserve more. We believe that somehow time, or God, or life in general, has cheated us out of what is rightfully ours. This is why we struggle with time. It's connected to our desires, and many times our desires are full of sin! We want the time to do everything we need to do, want to do, and feel we deserve to do. However, time is not the real problem. It feels like the problem is a lack of priorities. Maybe, it's time to look and listen closely at what is most important.

Our priorities are often jaded by our pasts. Our pasts tend to blur our futures. This is a dangerous combination. What most people do is try to use their pasts as an excuse for why they can't obtain the futures they desire most. We all have a tendency to let our pasts hold us back. What we should do, is use the past to learn for the future. No one has a perfect past, but that should not define the future. The reality is that the past provides invaluable insight into what's next.

These signs we hold up as badges of honor are more numerous than we can discuss. We think if we carry them around, they give us security or something to fall back on. The truth is that they provide nothing. They block our view of the future, and they skew the vision for the path that is being carved out for us. These are the collected signs that sit in the "garage" of our hearts and minds and take up so much wasted space. In reality, they serve no purpose. We discussed the two big ones, but there are so many more we use in our lives.

"Victim"

"Abandoned"

"Abused"

"Unloved" or "Unlovable"

"Single"

"Addict"

"Unforgiven"

"Poor" (in money and/or spirit)

WHAT SIGNS DO YOU HOLD AS A "BADGE OF HONOR"?

o _____

o _____

o _____

o _____

o _____

o _____

o _____

These combination signs and the signs we often hold up as badges of honor are real. There are millions of people who have been abused, neglected, abandoned, cheated on, lied to, and hurt. The hurt and the pain are absolutely real. My challenge is for us to use these feelings from our pasts to propel us to something greater in the future. Only God can take the pain away and allow us to forgive deeply. In truth, the pain will probably never leave us entirely. That doesn't mean, however, it needs to define us! We are more than what has happened to us. Paul, when writing his second letter to the Corinthians, started by encouraging those who have faced trials and hardships to understand that God would comfort them so that they can then comfort others (2 Corinthians 1:3-4). What we have learned from these challenges is exactly what someone else needs to hear.

I had an alcoholic father, who my mother had to tell to leave when my brother and I were two years old. I grew up without a dad. My mom did an amazing job raising my brother and me, with some special assistance from my grandparents. I learned from a young age to focus on what I had, and not what I had lost. I refused to let the lack of a father keep me from being a well-rounded young man, who could play sports with the best of them and also show his sensitive side. I have been able to connect with countless kids and adults in the last thirty-five years who don't have a father either, and I refuse to let them use this as an excuse that holds them back from the lives created for them! We all have areas of our lives that we probably wish had never happened. Yet, this makes us who we are. We live, we learn, and we share those lessons with others.

The one sign that we carry around that harms both our pasts and futures in the most dangerous and impactful ways is the "If I Only" badge.

We live in a sinful world where things rarely work out like anyone plans. There is real pain and suffering and sickness and death. There are people who say mean things, treat us with disrespect, and always want more than we feel we can offer. And this is just in our own families; forget about the rest of the world!

Somehow, we think our whole life would change completely "if only" we had made that one key decision. We make hundreds, if not thousands of decisions per day. Changing the one decision or moment does not guarantee we make perfect decisions from that point forward in our lives. The one decision or one moment would not provide us the perfectly smooth ride we often dream of at night.

Some decisions are pivotal. There is the time you didn't tell someone you loved them. You may mourn the time you made a really poor decision and broke a boundary or rule that left you with very strong consequences. You may still think about the time you should have pressed harder for something, or the time you should have simply said, "no." There are plenty of times when you should have loved deeper, asked for forgiveness, or shown grace to another human being. There are times where you sat on the sidelines when you should have gotten into the game. There are other times when you rushed full speed ahead and probably should have waited. Everyone makes mistakes.

When I was sixteen years old, one of my best friends died in a car accident. I was actually the last person to see him alive. I was coming up to a stop sign and waved as he turned onto the road. He overcorrected his car and ran head-on into a truck about four and a half miles later. The police said he died instantly. There were at least five thousand times in the following weeks that I wondered why I didn't wave him down more vigorously. I thought if I had stopped him or made him pause, even if just for a few seconds, I could have changed the outcome. Maybe, I could have alleviated all the pain and hurt for his family and his friends. His personality, charm, and charisma were contagious. He certainly was a changer of worlds.

WHAT ARE YOUR "IF ONLY" MOMENTS?

- _____

- _____

- _____

- _____

- _____

- _____

- _____

We all have these moments. I will not pretend to tell you they do not matter. I also cannot promise you that life would have worked out differently. Your life may have turned out worse. You could have fixed one problem, but created a dozen more to solve and question. Your life matters to you, but it matters to those around you as well. Your family, your friends, your co-workers, the neighbor across the street you rarely take time to say hello to, and the person in line in front of you, are all affected by your decisions.

One of my favorite movies is *About Time*. The general premise is that Domhnall Gleeson's character is able to travel back and forth in time to specific days in his life. He is able to redo embarrassing missteps and costly mistakes. While various parts of life are corrected, he is also able to learn that one cannot fix everything. In the end, he attempts to live each day with purpose and make the best of each moment. These attitudes and approaches change him so much, he stops going back in time at all. Our attitudes towards the moments of life, and our understanding of what we truly control, matters most. This is true for ourselves and for those we love. This is true for all of us. Even if we could travel back and do it differently, I am almost certain the end result would not be perfection.

I had to make peace with that myself as a sixteen-year-old kid. Why would God call such a great young man home at such an early age? Did I have a part to play in all of this, and did I do something wrong? I cried. I tried. I prayed. I wrestled with this over and over again, and could not make any sense or peace. Then, one day, God sent the sparrows. Literally, they came to the yard and sat in the trees and spoke to my soul. Over two thousand years ago, Jesus reminded His disciples that if God took care of the sparrows, their food and every detail of their life, why would He not take care of the details of our lives. Jesus was speaking the same message to my soul. It is not my job to fix that which is out of my control.

I did not understand the "why" of God. I didn't understand it then and I still do not understand it today. But I don't have to understand the "why" to live this life to the fullest. Corrie ten Boom, who suffered through a great many tragedies at the hands of Nazi Germany, said it best. When asked how she was able to make sense of all the death and the unbelievable circumstances that most would call unfair to say the least, she allegedly responded with the following statement, "I stopped trying to understand why God does what He does; instead I started focusing on learning more about who God is." This has become one of my all-time favorite quotes.

The best example of trying to understand the thought process of God comes in the book of Job. Job was a really neat guy who had it all going for him. He had a beautiful family, tons of possessions, and a passion for loving God. One day, God gave him the ultimate challenge. Job was charged with keeping his faith in God despite the harshest and most extreme losses imaginable. God allowed the devil to take it all away, every last person and thing Job loved in his life. Job was withered down to a sick and pitiful human being who lost his family, his wealth, and his health in a few hours of time. His friends told him to curse God and die. They told him none of this made any sense and he must be to blame. Job tried to keep his faith. The struggle was deep, and it was real.

Job told his friends that God was up to something. He shared that he did not understand it, but he trusted God was still working. He kept praying while struggling to keep his faith. Finally, he questioned God and really pushed in on the "why." God pushed back. He asked Job where he was when He made this whole world, the stars, the mountains, the oceans, and the creatures of the deep. He reminded Job of his own limitations, while boldly sharing that He has none. God allowed Job to catch a glimpse of His majesty, His wonder, and His power. Job fell to the ground and repented in dust and ashes (Job 40-42). Just a glimpse of the glory of God changed everything. He admitted that once he questioned God, he finally understood he had it all wrong. Job could never understand what God is up to each day. Job, just like each of us, could never fully understand and completely grasp the "why." Finally, Job admitted he had heard rumors of God and thought he knew Him, but since he saw Him "face to face," he was changed. Job understood God and understood grace more deeply. God restored Job completely. He actually gave

Job twice as much as He had initially. The pain and struggle were real. They stayed with Job all of his life. The reality of the splendor, majesty, and sheer awesomeness of God stayed with him too.

Everything is settled for Job. I wish it were that easy for us to settle this in our lives as well. It is not our own understanding that will allow us to throw away the "If Only" sign. It is trusting in the glory of an almighty God who holds the world, even the sparrows, in His hand. It is having faith to know God has plans for us that we have never seen or imagined. It is believing that allowing God to take control of the wheel is the safest and best place we can be in our story. It's also the place where we get to go on the ride of our lives.

This is the intersection of faith, and it's staring you down. You must decide what you are going to do with it. Are you going to attempt to control everything, or are you going to let go? It's all an illusion anyway. There is no real control. You cannot make anyone do the slightest thing. You don't control the weather, if your dog is going to wake you up barking, or the behavior of others in traffic. You cannot tell if you will get sick today or protect someone close to you from falling ill. You cannot make someone be nice to you, forgive you, or love you. You have no control over the Major League Baseball game, the next global health pandemic, or what the Dow futures hold.

5

FEAR OF TODAY VS.
FAITH FOREVER

I refuse to watch any scary movies. The world is scary enough. I like comedies a lot, but what I love most is a great love story with rising action, a few laugh out loud moments, a plot twist that I knew was coming but still slightly surprised me, and of course, a happy ending. I think I like them most because they are predictable and controlled. Even though I may doubt for a few moments if it's going to all work out, I know deep down everything is going to be alright in the end. In case you haven't figured it out yet, we watch movies; we don't get to live them. We don't get to control the end outcomes. There is no promise or guarantee everything is going to turn out as expected in life. We make plans, but we have to trust the Lord to direct our steps and adjust our course (Proverbs 16:9).

I cannot live in fear. My pastor, Nick Newman, loves to say, "The opposite of fear is not faith. The opposite of fear is courage." Courage is being scared to do something but going ahead and doing it anyway. The strongest courage is displayed when you can step out in faith to do something and truly have no idea which way it is going to go. You realize you do not control the final outcome and cannot predict the happy ending, but you go forward in faith anyway.

Jim Elliot lived the greatest example of courage I have ever read. Knowing God wanted him and his colleagues to reach an unreached people with the gospel of Jesus Christ, they set out on a most courageous journey. They prayed and planned and made contact with the Auca/Waodani tribe of Ecuador. They dropped gifts and attempted to show themselves as peaceful and wanting to connect. Initially, things went really well. They were able to land their small plane on the river near the village. They met with a few of the tribesmen and women. The missionaries were able to make contact and were so excited to come back. The men made plans to reconnect. They landed their small plan and were ready to meet with about ten tribesmen. In a moment, everything changed. According to the story, some members of the tribe were scared and skeptical and did not believe the missionaries' motives. The very group they were trying to love, killed all five men and threw their bodies in the river. Jim Elliot was twenty-eight years old. He left behind a wife and an eleven-month-old daughter. It was a tragedy, and it made little sense. How could God allow this to happen when they were following His lead of love? They were doing His work and following His will.

Jim's wife shared the story. She shared this story of boldness and courage and faith because she knew God was not finished. Eventually, she and another one of the deceaseds' family members were able to reach this group. God allowed the tribe to hear about the love, grace, forgiveness, and eternal life that is only found in Jesus. They experienced this firsthand as Jim's wife forgave the very men who killed her husband. Another man, Nate Saint, was killed on that riverbank as well. His son, Steve, lived with the Auca/Waodoni tribe for years. He was "adopted" into their culture. Mincaye, one of the men who helped kill Nate's father and the other men, accepted Christ and His love. Mincaye and Steve became great friends and traveled the world sharing this true redemption story. These stories have been shared countless times as an example of how faith and courage intersect and how God is always working in every circumstance. What did not make sense at the time has now been a calling card for missionaries and Christians everywhere all over the world. It has led to millions of people worldwide hearing the good news that Jesus offers us all.

Courage really begins with acknowledging your fears. Everyone has them, and most of us are scared to name or admit them. One of the greatest ways fear takes hold is that it stays in the background and hides under the surface. Fear will try to convince you not to give it a name or an identity. This is a key power play that fear creates in your life. Write down your fears, pick at least five of your deepest and darkest. By naming your fears, you have the opportunity to make them real. It sounds counterproductive, but naming your fears and making them real is the only way to face them head-on with faith and courage.

LIST THE REAL FEARS IN YOUR LIFE TODAY.

○ _____

○ _____

○ _____

○ _____

○ _____

○ _____

○ _____

Now that you have named your fears, you must decide what you are going to do with them. Do you let them have control? Do you let them steal your joy? Do your fears dictate your attitude, your reactions, and your responses to the day? Think about which fears that you control. Do you really have control over them, or is it an illusion of control?

One of the greatest joys of life is watching kids grow up. What people often do not share is that allowing them to grow up and struggle is scary. I know in my life, I have overreacted in my response to my kids based out of fear more often than I would like to admit. I want my kids to grow up to be world-changers! Yet, I let fear keep me from always letting them step out in faith and step into the struggle. I hold them back more often than I should because I let fear creep in and fill my head and heart with doubt.

If you are a parent, you have probably done this as well. Sometimes, it is innocent enough. You don't want them to wander too far on the playground, so you call them back or run after them. You don't want them to fall out of the tree, so you tell them to stop at the second branch. You don't want them to bust their head, so you make them stop flipping from bed to bed in the hotel room. All of these reactions are completely logical, and these behaviors absolutely should be addressed. Although, how we respond to them and how we teach fear to our kids is key.

Let's analyze the tree-climbing example a little deeper. My son still loves to climb trees at fifteen-years old. We went for a quick trip to the beach and rode bike trails with a group of people. He was in the front and I was in the back with the younger kids. We had to stop for a bridge. By the time I caught up from the back, he had gotten bored waiting for thirty seconds and was twenty feet up in a tree. Why not? Thankfully, I figured at fifteen, he could handle it and didn't say a word. This wasn't always the case.

When he was little, he used to love to climb a dogwood tree at the home of my wife's parents. Dogwoods are great for climbing because they have low branches. However, I was always quick to remind him to be careful, stop him from climbing too far, or move to stand right underneath the tree. I wanted him to be adventurous and courageous, as all kids should be, but I also wanted a guarantee that a trip to the emergency room was not going to be required. Isn't this how a lot of us approach life? We want to face our fears and throw caution to the wind, but we want the guaranteed promise that nothing too bad will happen to us if we do. We want to take the job with the new startup company that is a perfect fit for our gifts and talents, but only if we have a large amount in savings and a guaranteed contract if the company should fail. We deeply desire to serve more and give more time to our church or community, but only if it does not interfere with our preplanned family activities.

Do you know what I learned most from all of the struggle, fear and work that I put into focusing on him climbing the tree? My son wasn't listening to me. I came to pick him up one day, and he had fallen out of the tree. Thank the Lord, he didn't have any broken bones! He did have some scratches, two knots, and one really cool story. Even if he had broken his arm, it would have only made his story that much cooler. Another day I came to pick him up and stopped my car as I turned into the driveway. He was literally standing at the top of the tree waving above the carport from about sixteen feet up. That was another great story. My fear did not change his behavior or the outcome.

Letting fear lead did not help when I taught our daughter to ride a bike, when we bought them a trampoline, and when we let them go on a mission trip halfway across the country without us. My fear did not change their behaviors or the outcome. Modeling how to ride a bike, jump appropriately, and love all people changed the outcome. Encouragement, guidance, and working to try to impart wisdom made a difference. Teaching them a healthy respect of fear and trying to prayerfully find the balance with this emotion made a difference. Praying for our children changed the outcome. Having a calm conversation in the truck on the way to dinner changed the outcome. Overreacting and letting fear take the lead did not help one bit.

Fear is real in our own lives, and often takes hold over the lives of those we love as well. We often justify that our fear is appropriate because we care so much. I have done this many times as well. We argue that we just want our kids to grow up the right way and to be the best they can be. We are afraid we will do something that will knock them off this path. But the truth is, perfect love drives out fear (I John 4:18). There is no greater love than the love of Jesus. All of us, you and me, are His children. We are the most wonderful creation of God the Father and we were created in and through Jesus. Jesus prayed for us, for you and for me, in His greatest moments of fear (John 17). He did not let fear take the lead in the garden of Gethsemane or on the cross. He loves us with an everlasting love. If He did not fear in those times, then why should we fear in love? Fear creates doubt, uncertainty, anger, confusion, and destruction. Often times, our fear as parents creates this for our kids as well. This is knocks them off their paths quicker than anything else. It is difficult, but we must place fear behind us. Throw it out with the other signs we have created, collected, and become far too comfortable using.

We all have someone that we love deeply. We are created to be relational beings who thrive on connecting with others. In any relationship, we must commit to living in love and letting go of fear. The fruits of the Spirit are love, joy, peace, patience, kindness, goodness, faithfulness, gentleness, and self-control (Galatians 5:22-23). These are connected at every level. Love, gentleness, and kindness create peace, patience, and self-control. In the same way, gentleness, self-control, and patience create more opportunities to love and the ability to share, show kindness, and be peace in the lives of others. The final truth is that realizing if we fill ourselves completely with these fruits, there is very little room left for fear to take root. We can overwhelm our relationships with all of these pieces and force fear to flee.

We must learn from our past. Remember, our goal is to permanently get rid of the signs that have been defining us. We have all made mistakes. We all have reacted in fear and let uncertainty or anger dictate a time or even a season of our relationships. This is the past. It is over. If we have taken the ride with Jesus, it is forgiven. God knows we will not get it right every time. Our kids know this truth as well. Every person we encounter in every relationship has an innate understanding that there are times where one or both of us will make a mess of a conversation, interaction, and relationship. Any relationship with any other person is never perfect.

While our ultimate goal is to overwhelm our relationships with the fruits of the Spirit, we must also take time to celebrate progress. Anytime our initial reaction is love or peace, we are making progress. Anytime we are able to react differently in peace, say something differently in love, or do something differently with more gentleness, we are moving closer to the goal of all relationships. Progress allows us to move from what is good, towards something better, and ultimately, to what is best. This "good, better, best" model is one of the biggest measuring sticks to remove the signs of fear that we hold. This model will allow us to focus on our progress towards freedom. The fruits of the Spirit will help us lay down our own signs as we release the power those signs have held over us.

The extraordinary life is one that is led by love. Love allows courage to take hold of our fears. I attended the NC Baptist Mission Conference last year, where our theme was "Known by Love." This is a powerful statement and goal. It also makes a very powerful sign. Think about what would happen if every word, every interaction, every purpose in your life towards any person, was completely dictated by love. The power of love can never be underestimated. Huey Lewis taught me that in the movie *Back to the Future*. (Watch it and you'll understand.) We do not control much in this life, but we can control our actions of love. Let's make a commitment to show more love. Make a commitment to be known by love and embrace our progress in this area. The rest of what is out of our control, we must give to Jesus. We place the unseen and the unknown in the hands of Jesus. We leave them there with Him. After all, I would much rather keep my plans in His hands, the One who created it all and keeps His promises and faith forever, than keep them in my own (Psalm 146:6).

Let's take time to review where we have been in this section. I hope you have learned that the signs you are carrying around are weighing you down in so many ways. The person you see in the mirror is not defined by their looks. The person you see in the mirror is not defined by their past. The person you see in the mirror cannot change by themselves. That person is being changed and renewed day by day. They are no longer defined by the signs they have created, became too comfortable with, or collected along the way. The person in the mirror is no longer going to be defined by their signs, their past, or their fear. The person is the mirror is making progress to be known by love.

HOW ARE YOU CHANGING?

- ○ --
- ○ --
- ○ --
- ○ --
- ○ --
- ○ --
- ○ --

SECTION 2

TURNING YOUR SIGN INTO A STORY

Do you remember when you were a little kid and you always had to ask permission to do something? It did not matter what it was, once you had obtained permission, it was full speed ahead. You need to learn to give yourself permission. You must allow yourself to let go of your signs and let go of your past. You have become stuck or even trapped in routines and cycles that keep you from fulfilling what is still within your reach. You need to allow yourself permission to open your mind to new ideas and new possibilities. You need to awaken the "inner-child" excitement and get on with your life and your story. Do not stay still. You have permission to run free and embrace what is waiting for you and your story.

Robert Frost was an unknown, aspiring poet living in America. In 1910, at forty years of age, he gave himself permission to sell his dairy farm and move his wife and family to England, where he had heard they might be more receptive to the poems he enjoyed writing. Many of us would argue this was expected of Robert Frost. After all, he was the very poet who coined the most searched poem in the history of Google. Surely, he had this inside of him his whole life. This absolutely would have been his road "less traveled by." This behavior should be expected by someone who was willing to travel a different path. Here is the catch, and it is one that we cannot miss. "The Road Not Taken" by Robert Frost is arguably the most misunderstood and misquoted poem in the history of poetry. Frost reportedly wrote this poem for a friend. His goal was to show his friend (and many more still today who need this reminder) that both roads were equal. There was not a right or a wrong choice. The choice that "made all the difference," was only in the mind of the person. Robert Frost did not want us holding up our signs either! He wanted us to understand that we make choices in our lives, frame them in certain ways, and give them too much power. Life is bigger than one choice. No matter which choices we make, they do not have to define the future of our lives.

Let's take the road. Which road one might ask? Take any road. Commit to leaving the past behind. You are going to leave your past thoughts, the past vision of yourself, your perceived limitations, your "if only" moments, and of course, the signs you have collected, created, and used for comfort. You will no longer allow your signs and past to provide excuses in your life. You are going to move forward. You are going to take steps towards what is next.

You are more than a sign. You are a story. You are not defined by singular moments. All of your life is knit and pieced together to create a story. It is time to starting writing and living the best story, because it is the story of you! This is your story. It is time to understand that your story is worth being lived and shared in its entirety.

WHAT ARE SOME RISKS THAT YOU WOULD LIKE TO TAKE OR GOALS YOU WOULD LIKE TO ACCOMPLISH? HOLD NOTHING BACK.

- ○ _____

- ○ _____

- ○ _____

- ○ _____

- ○ _____

- ○ _____

- ○ _____

6

TAKE THE ROAD

In high school, I wrote a biography about my grandfather. His story was incredible. I knew his story as "grandpa," the man who I thought hung the moon. He was kind and gentle, but also strong and confident. He taught me how to grow the best garden and shoot a left-handed layup with ease. Most importantly, he taught me the best life lessons on love, kindness, and generosity because he lived them out every single moment of his life. The story he rarely ever mentioned was the fact that he should have never made it to become my grandfather. At twenty-three years old, while serving our country in WWII off the coast of New Guinea, his ship was struck by a Japanese "kamikaze" airplane. He survived in the ocean for sixteen hours, swallowing oil and fire in the process. His fifteen-month recovery in New Mexico cost him a lung and a giant scar that stretched from the back of his shoulder blade around to his abdomen. One day, while he was in the hospital, all the windows blew out and the hospital shook for several minutes. He later learned that he had just experienced the first atomic bomb testing.

He married his beautiful bride of sixty-four years less than a year later. He managed the National Shirt and Hat Shop in downtown Winston-Salem, NC, and retired early to spend time with his kids. He was the best grandfather a boy could ever imagine and shaped the story of my life in ways I cannot even describe or probably fathom. He was the godliest man because of how he cared for others. He was a servant-husband, servant-leader, and a man everyone admired.

He rarely talked about these past parts of his story. His past had shaped him, but it never defined him. He lived each day as if it was a gift. He enjoyed life and embraced each opportunity that the day might present. He always loved to tell me, "Don't put off until tomorrow, what you could do today." I'm pretty sure he made that commitment in the Pacific Ocean that day in 1944, deciding to live life to the fullest each and every day. He lived his story one day a time. He put his best out there each day of his life. He took whatever road the day provided and walked forward, allowing his steps to be known by love. He didn't talk much about his story; he lived it, every single day.

What I love most about real-life examples are the glimpse that they provide us into how we can live our own story. They offer encouragement and challenges to remind us that our story is also waiting. Peter had a lot going for him. He was passionate, driven, committed, willing to take risks, and bold. He had some great qualities and was living his story. He was showing himself as a devoted follower of Jesus, his teacher, Lord, and friend. Peter was making all the right moves. Until one day, he took a step that threatened to derail his story completely. Think about your worst mistake and multiply it by infinity. Peter literally cussed out a young girl and group around a fire and denied even knowing Jesus. Of course, this was when Jesus, his Lord and friend, needed him the most. Peter wept (Matthew 26:75). I would have too. It would have been one of those moments that there was no recovering from and absolutely no way back. Do you have one of those moments? Is it heavy and weighing you down? Has it become a sign that you feel you may never lose? When we blow it royally, especially when it hurts someone we love, it always seems so final. Only, with Jesus, nothing is ever final.

Jesus rose from the grave (John 20). He defeated death and sin and also our worst mistakes. One morning after His resurrection, Jesus came to show Peter over breakfast, how He overcame it all. Jesus found Peter on a boat holding his old "fisherman" sign and called out to him. Once Peter realized who it was, he jumped in the water with reckless abandon. He could not get to Jesus quick enough. Jesus talked to Peter and asked him three times, "Do you love me?" Jesus wasn't being a jerk. He wanted to show Peter that He could restore any mistake. Jesus allowed Peter to repeat his love for Him three times, to show that he was forgiven for each denial, and to remind him of the greatest love (John 21). Then, Jesus challenged Peter to choose a road paved with love and serving. He wanted Peter to follow Him in serving and loving others with the same reckless abandon that he jumped out of the boat with a few moments earlier. Jesus reminded Peter that it was his choice.

Peter and Jesus finished breakfast. I can only imagine how joyful and relieved Peter must have felt. Then, something interesting happens. Peter looked over and saw another disciple and good friend, John. Peter looked towards Jesus and asked, "What about him?" Now, I will not pretend to know why Peter was worried about John. I wonder if he expected Jesus to challenge John in the same manner. I wonder if Peter wanted to know if John was going to go with him on this journey. I wonder if Peter wanted some insight into what John was going to be doing or where he would go from that point forward with his own story. Jesus responded, "What is it to you? If I want John to remain until I come, what does it matter to you?" Then, Jesus said a statement we cannot miss, "*YOU* follow Me" (John 21:22, emphasis added).

Your journey, your signs, your story, your future, your path, your love, and your God-ordained plan are yours alone. It does not matter what someone else may say or do, or which path they choose to follow. They may be on a great path. Someone else may be doing everything right and living a life of love to the fullest. That is wonderful for them. That is their journey and their story. I pray that they have overcome their signs and are living out their story. What you need to desperately see in this moment is the power of your story lies solely in the fact that it is YOURS! Only you will meet certain people on your path to love. Only you will be able to overcome certain conditions or circumstances, which you will then share with others so that they may overcome as well. Only you will be able to be the husband or wife or mother or father or son or daughter or friend or coworker others will need. This is your story. It must always remain your story.

You have been given this one life to live. You have been challenged by Jesus Himself and the God of the universe to step out and live your story, because you are the only one who can do it. Jesus didn't talk to John about loving people, following Him, and feeding His sheep. It didn't mean that Jesus did not want John to do these things, but that particular challenge and restoration was Peter's story. That was his challenge and his alone. Before you can go any further, you must come to a peace that your story is purposefully yours. What has happened in the past is yours, and what will happen in the future is yours. It can be exciting or scary or overwhelming or all three at once, but it is a marvelous privilege as well. The God of all creation has a story for you to live, not just write. Take the road He has laid before you. Make the commitment to live it well.

7

TAKE THE REALITY

In a world of virtual reality, distorted reality, glamorous social media posts, and too many false realities to count, it can be quite difficult to discern your true reality. Your story and true reality go hand-in-hand. One major reason many people struggle to live their story is because they will not accept their reality. The reality of your story is extraordinary.

I am asking you to dive deeper into your life so that you can deeply discover your own story. You must begin to view your life as a story that is worth being lived and worth being shared. Your story is just as valuable and important as any social media celebrity. This is reality. You are so much more than what you allow others to see and are more than worthy of sharing your story. Your story adds value to so many other stories around you. Even as I make this statement, there is probably a voice inside your head telling you this is not true. We are our own worst enemies. Give yourself permission to believe your story is incredible and valuable, because it absolutely is! Dr. Seuss said it best, "There is only one you!" This is by design.

WHAT AREAS OF YOUR LIFE ARE WORTH
BEING SHARED WITH OTHERS?

o   _____

o   _____

o   _____

o   _____

o   _____

o   _____

o   _____

Let's revisit the mirror. We started our journey together by standing in front of the mirror. Go back there for a moment. There are three types of people you see in the mirror. There is the "you" people think you are, the "you" that you believe you are, and the "you" you were created to be!

There is no greater example than the story of a young man named David. David looked in the mirror each morning before he went to work his mundane job. I do not know which "you" David saw in his reflection. It may have depended on the day. Everyone else pretty much looked at David as the youngest and least talented in the family. He made a slight name for himself as a "pretty good shepherd," but that's like being the tallest guy in the Napoleon basketball league. In the eyes of others, David left a lot to be desired. In God's eyes, David was living his story perfectly. God was training and preparing David for his future, even in the mundane moments. The prophet Samuel reminded everyone, "Man looks at the outward appearance, but God looks at the heart" (1 Samuel 16:7).

When you look at yourself, how often do you look at your heart? Your heart is the wellspring, or source, of life (Proverbs 4:23). Your heart will lead you in love. Your heart will remind you of what's really important. It will encourage you and ground you. It will remind you of how deep and wide and great God's love is for you.

David had to know there was something more inside of him. He had to trust and look at his own heart as well. Some may call it the "call of the wild," but I prefer to think of it as the call of his soul. Our souls constantly call us to remember that we are more. We have more inside of us than we can ever imagine. We have more to offer others than we believe is possible. We have more to learn, more to receive, more to embrace, and more to do. What we see and what others see is never what God sees! David's soul must have called him to remember that God gave him a story to live and to share. God saw David for both what he was, and for what he would become. David looked deep inside to his own heart and soul. The rest, as they say, is history.

David allowed God to awaken the story inside of him. This caused him to better understand that his purpose was far greater and his story more magnificent than he could ever have imagined. The defeat of the giant Goliath with just a sling and some stones was only the beginning. His story took him to the greatest heights as the king of all Israel. It also took him to some deep lows. David wrote the most amazing songs, or psalms, about the greatness, faithfulness, and everlasting love of God. David's story was a grand story because it was focused on God's never-ending pursuit and faithfulness in the eternal promises to him.

David's story was not an easy story. It was a grand story that took David to places he would have never imagined. It caused David to question God, experience the wonders of God, and have the fullness of faith that allowed him to follow God wherever He would lead. David's story was anything from a smooth, straight path. It was a winding road that sometimes veered off course, but ultimately allowed David to be called a man after God's own heart. His pursuit of God—the promises, fullness, and great love of God—kept pushing him back on track. This allowed David to keep living his story boldly and walking in faith.

Your story should be the same. Have you ever really wondered what is down deep inside your soul? Five, ten, twenty-five, or fifty years from now, what will your story say? It does not matter how many curves and how winding your road has been to this point. God can use all of your past in any way He chooses. You can learn lessons, share your past with others, or be reminded over and over again that it does not define you. You are being made new every, single day and being covered in the love and grace of Jesus. He is pushing you forward to a new day and a call to "follow Me."

You have a story to live loudly. Your journey is not one that you travel alone. There are others depending on you, needing you, and watching you. Your story is wrapped up in the lives of others. Other people need you to live your story. Think about what you have to offer those around you. Can you afford to stop your story now?

If you have a story to share with the world, then you must come to grips with a deep truth. Your story is not going to turn out like you think it will. This is great news! The story you have told yourself and you think others will see is nothing like the story God has prepared for you.

IF YOU ARE GOING TO SHARE YOUR STORY, WHAT DO YOU WISH GOD WOULD REVEAL TO YOU? WHAT DO YOU WANT HIM TO SHOW YOU? WHAT WOULD MAKE YOU FEEL MORE CONFIDENT ABOUT YOUR OWN STORY?

- _____
- _____
- _____
- _____
- _____
- _____
- _____

When I was a teenager, I distinctly remember sitting in my bedroom thinking, "God, if you would just go ahead and show me a few dates on this timeline of life, I would feel so much better about things." I wanted a glimpse of me working for _Sports Illustrated_, watching my bride walk down the aisle, and still being active and excited at age seventy-two. These images were comforting to me. In my mind, they were assurances that my life was going to turn out really well. They were moments that would keep me focused and moving forward to my goals. It all sounded good. Of course, it did not happen. This type of security seems well and good, but that's not living life in faith. There is no faith, no trust, and no reason to passionately pursue that which we hope lies in front of us.

I did get to watch my beautiful bride walk down the aisle and have been married to her for over twenty years! It has been the most wonderful journey. It has not been easy, but it has been extraordinary, filled with grace and forgiveness, and has led us to some amazing highs as well as some frustrating lows. I can honestly say that I love her as much now, much farther down the road in our journey, than I did when we took the first step. I thank God for bringing us together and keeping us together, but guess what I love most? Her. I love her! This only works because it is our story! I could never live out this story with anyone else. To paraphrase *Jerry Maguire*, she completes me. She is the only one who can. Someone else would never help me write my story this way. This is why your story is so innately powerful. It lies inside of you alone.

I did not get to write for *Sports Illustrated*. I did write for my college newspaper. I've written a few songs, a couple articles for magazines, and have struggled consistently with writing my blog (signtostory.org). I would not be considered a professional writer. However, I did get to teach second graders how to write powerful stories. I helped fifth graders write poetry and thank you notes to their families for graduation. I wrote papers in college to prepare to be a principal. I handwrite individual notes to every teacher at the beginning of each semester, reminding them of the impact they make every single day. I'm currently writing this book. God did use me to write, but not in the way I envisioned. I would not change a thing! Being a principal, which allows me to support and love on kids, teachers, and staff, is the greatest joy I could ever imagine. I would never trade writing for *Sports Illustrated* over serving and leading the most amazing school.

Had God given me a glimpse of an older me sitting at a desk with pictures of famous athletes surrounding me on every side, I would have never imagined becoming a teacher and principal. I would not have committed to educating and impacting the lives of thousands of children. My story would have stopped short of where God intended. I would have never taken the risks of having a smaller salary, lack of bonuses, lower reputation, and ability to hang out with the coolest five- and ten-year-olds instead of sports superstars. I would have missed out on so much. My story is different than I imagined, and that is a beautiful and comforting thought and truth.

How do you feel about your story right now? Are you where you thought you would be in your story? Regardless of whether you are right where imagined you would be in your life or miles away from any directional guideposts, God will meet you right where you currently sit. Wherever you are in your story, God is near.

TAKE THE RIDE

Right now, you may be thinking that your life is the farthest thing from a story that someone would want to read or watch. Let me challenge you with a thought. Think about a journey you have been on in your life. It could be a four-hour journey to the beach, a two-week mission trip, a journey through a new career, or the journey of becoming a spouse, mother, or father. Each journey has its ups and downs, its trying hills, and its jarring speed bumps. It also may have its mountain tops and epic ending. Your life is the same!

You must accept the journey. When you accept it, the journey will take you places you have never imagined as your story starts to take shape. Every real story has drama, rising action, conflict, struggle, inner turmoil, and a happily ever after. These are the elements that make a great story. Why do you think they would not be included in yours? If you are taking the ride, leaving your signs, and living out your story, it will be full of struggles and turmoil. These will shape your story. Like your signs, they cannot define you. They should only shape you and propel you forward.

Everything in life is a growth experience. You must remember the struggle and embrace it. You must seize the opportunity to grow. Growth cannot occur on your own. You must have someone to propel you forward and something that causes you to embrace the struggle. This is where faith steps into our stories. Faith was given to us by God. It is wrapped up completely in Him. Faith calls us to remember the best is yet to come. It is that desire, deep down in your soul, to believe in what has not happened yet. This feeling is faith wanting to act. It is the belief more is possible and more of your story is waiting. However, you must be willing to move and lead your story to a new season, a new opportunity, or a new destination. Anyone who ever took the next step, took it towards something.

WHAT ARE YOU MOVING TOWARDS?

- _____

- _____

- _____

- _____

- _____

- _____

- _____

If you are going to move forward and face your reality, take a mustard seed with you. You have probably never seen a mustard seed before because they are extremely small. They also don't work well on hot dogs. Jesus said if you have faith the size of a mustard seed, you can move mountains (Matthew 17:20). I like to think He meant that you would not let anything stop you or stand in your way on your journey as you live your story. If faith can move mountains, it can absolutely help you overcome obstacles along the way. There will always be the struggles and the turmoil that attempt to hold you back. Struggle can take the form of a person, an action, a sign, or a stronghold. Turmoil may exist as an addiction or a relationship. Struggles and turmoil may find you suddenly, or they may have been there for a while. These are the things you must move past if you are to take the ride. Faith is what allows you to move them, even if it just means moving past them before they move completely.

Faith always propels you forward. Fear is what will drive you backwards. Think about a time when you took a risk and faced your reality. I can promise that your outcome and the outcome you desired were not something in the past. There are so many stories that showcase faith, but faith is also very personal. You cannot borrow faith from someone else. Faith cannot be tricked. Faith must be embraced and owned. Like your story, your faith is yours alone.

The Bible says that each person has a manner, or amount, of faith (Romans 12:3). Of all the people that I have met in my entire life, I have yet to meet two people who have an equal amount of faith. Most people will tell you they believe in God. It really is hard to pause, look around and see all the beauty this world contains, and believe there is no God. After our son was born and I observed the miracle of life firsthand, I immediately thought if anyone could watch the birth of a child and not believe in a God who designs, creates, and gives us life, they must be completely blind.

The day our son was born required a huge amount of faith. Everyone typically loves to talk about the day their child was born. Except, they don't really talk about the day. They pull out five to seven minutes of the exciting parts, and leave out the twenty hours of waiting, praying, and listening to a heart monitor beat constantly. I am not even going to start to pretend I had the worst job, but being an "almost" dad on the day of your child's birth is super tough. I legitimately cannot even imagine being the one giving birth!

My wife Kristy had been in labor for about twelve hours when I started getting more anxious. Everything had stalled, and she wasn't feeling great. The doctor said they would check back in two hours and we might have to discuss options. I knew this meant a potential C-section and more trauma for Kristy and our son. I remember walking the halls of the maternity ward, praying, and wrestling with how little I controlled in this situation. I asked God for strength and protection over Kristy and our son, and asked Him for peace for us all. I also pushed hard for an answer and something for my faith to grab hold of during this time.

There are times when I distinctly hear God's voice in my life. I would love to tell you that it happens often, but I only get those moments at the mountaintops. I distinctly heard God speak to let me know to trust His timing and wait. He told me to wait until 10:00. It was around 6:40 in the evening, but I knew God was working, and that was all I needed. Around 8:45, the nurse came to check Kristy and felt there was finally progress being made. She said she would be back in about thirty minutes. By this time, Kristy was in full labor. Our nurse, who, praise God, was a church friend, was paging the doctor to come quickly. The rest was a blur. Before I knew it, our own miracle came into this world. I remember asking if everything was okay, trying to take the moment in, and double checking that his scrunched-up face and somewhat slimy appearance was normal. When it was finally over, I looked over at the clock. It read 10:07. I turned and asked our nurse, "What was his exact time of birth?" You can check his birth certificate. It was exactly 10:00. My faith grew tremendously on that day and in that exact moment.

My faith allowed me to look forward to a promise and to a moment. Faith supplied courage, assurance, comfort, peace, direction, and patience. It supplied all I needed at every level. The best description of faith is the original and biblical definition. Faith is the assurance of things hoped even though it is not yet seen or visible (Hebrews 11:1). Faith is believing the promise before it is seen. Faith is knowing the next step will produce results. Faith is what calls us to follow the light, no matter how dim, and to believe what's at the top of the mountain is worth the climb.

Faith must be the fuel for your story. It means taking the ride of your life and living your story, because you know where you are heading matters. No one gets all the assurances they want in life. No one is promised a smooth ride. God affirms our faith and allows us moments, like the day of our son's birth, to grow our faith. Faith is not magic, but it is powerful and purposeful in every aspect of our story. It allows us to grasp a deeper sense of ourselves. Faith allows us to be vulnerable and real, and serves as a constant reminder the best is yet to come.

If you have faith in God, you must believe He created you for a purpose. You must believe that the story He has called you to and created you for is needing to be lived. You keep stepping out in faith, and you keep trusting in every season of the journey. You embrace each piece of the story, and you commit to growing through it. You understand your story can only be really lived in faith. Faith is what gets you through each part, both good and bad, of your story. At the end of everyone's life, only three things remain—faith, hope, and love (1 Corinthians 13:13). Your story is best lived if all three pieces are seen throughout your entire life and story.

Faith calls us to do crazy things. I'm not referring to jumping off the bridge into the river or driving 130 mph, and praying nothing bad will happen. Even Jesus told the devil that one does not put God to a test (Matthew 4:7). I mean crazy things like quit one's lucrative job and pack up one's fifteen-year-old son and seven-year-old daughter to move to Brazil because the people there have never heard about this Jesus guy that can change their stories completely. It sounds crazy, but it is exactly what some friends of ours did two years ago.

After going on a few mission trips with our church team to Brazil, God spoke to them too. He told my friend to give up his general contracting business and move into a house about 1/7 of the size of their current house, which was also in the middle of a rainforest. God needed them to learn Portuguese enough to share all of the stories about Jesus too. Their entire world was going to change instantly. Faith was calling them to change their world, so that they could change the world of others. Their story just took a massive detour, and faith was the driver. They are now almost two years into this part of their story, and I wish you could sit down and hear the passion with which they speak about it. They do not talk about what they miss. Instead, they share about the opportunities they now have to love on people who look different, sound different, and act different, but need the love of Jesus, just like each and every one of us.

Faith not only gives us the encouragement and ability to live out our own stories; it also adjusts our stories and allows us to live our lives to the fullest. In my personal opinion, there is no greater example of faith than the story of a giant boat. Noah had a lot of positive things going on in his life. He had a strong family, with three sons to carry on his name. He loved the Lord and probably had a pretty solid reputation within his community. His story was going pretty well. Then, God changed his story from ordinary into extraordinary.

The Bible does not tell us about Noah before the boat, except to let us know that he loved God. Noah loved God so much that he reminded God of what was right with the world and humankind, and even why God had created people in the first place. Noah showed God there was at least one man left who had faith in Him. God saw Noah's love and faith, and revealed to him a deeper purpose and the next grand step in his story (Genesis 6:7-14).

In an instant, everything changed. God challenged Noah to embrace his story at an entirely new level. Noah's signs were replaced with a grand story. Noah received directions on how to build a boat, and a whole lot of jeers and laughter. He spent countless days building a giant ark to hold his family and every animal you can imagine, even the ones you wish he would have forgotten. The faith aspect really kicks through understanding that Noah had probably never seen rain before. When God made the world perfectly, everything worked, well, perfectly (Genesis 2:5-6). As sin continued to tear down what God had made, changes had to occur. Rain and flooding were two of those changes.

WHAT HAS GOD CALLED YOU TO DO BEFORE
THAT REQUIRED REAL, DEEP FAITH?

o _____

o _____

o _____

o _____

o _____

o _____

Noah just focused on the work. He did not let anything distract him. The signs of "What If...", "I Just Don't Understand," and "This Will Never Work" were moved completely out of the way. Two of Noah's greatest accomplishments were staying focused on what God asked of him and refusing to accept a sign by listening to anyone else.

If you are going to live your story in faith and live out the story God has prepared for you, then you must learn to leave behind the sign of another person's advice! Most people mean well, but some people are just mean. Many will share their opinions and advice freely, and often with what they believe are good intentions. The problem is that all of these other people do not know your story. They do not know what God has shared with you. They do not know your gifts and talents like God knows them. The tricky part is understanding that many well-meaning people will deter you from living your story in faith. It is not always the scoffers, mockers, and "haters." People around you don't want to see you "get hurt," make "financially unwise" decisions, or "waste" your abilities when you could be doing something so much more with your life. Don't pick up their signs. When you stay focused on God and His vision of your story, nothing is ever wasted.

This boat building was a massive undertaking. I am truly impressed with Noah's wife during this time. My wife has the God-given ability to help me stay focused and not waste time doing things, like watching too much football. She is a consummate professional at reminding me of how to prioritize my day and what to focus on in the moment. Some people may call this "nagging," but I call it a gift! In all seriousness, she truly does help me not waste my life on less important things. Noah's wife must have had tremendous faith too. The doubts had to creep up in the back of her mind. I'm sure she had to bite her tongue. I wonder how she wrestled with the whole scenario. I'm quite positive she really had to question what both God, and her husband, were exactly up to with this whole gigantic boat idea.

Noah's story is incredible. Noah, his family, and all of the animals survived for day after day and night after night on the boat with no promise of when it would all end. The nights were probably the hardest. They always are. When our kids were little and they would get sick, the nights were awful. The fever would spike, and they were restless. It felt like the darkness would last forever. I cannot imagine being tossed back and forth on a boat with no shred of light (a fire is really out of the question if one is on a completely wooden vessel with lots of swaying and rocking).

Your story will have nights as well. There are times when you feel the darkness lasts too long. There are times in your story when the darkness is overwhelming. The nights help shape the days. If you survive the nights and keep your faith pushing you forward, it makes the daylight so much sweeter.

One of my favorite songs of all-time is quite obscure and by the band *Brave Saint Saturn*. The name of the song is "Daylight." It tells the story of astronauts ascending on a mission to space, and the opening line reveals that there is a problem. They become lost in space with little hope for survival. The biggest problem for the astronauts is the fact they are stuck in an eclipse and have lost the daylight. It's one of my favorite songs because it is so real. I've never been to space, but I do sometimes feel lost.

Right now, you are trying to navigate the path you are on every day. The truth remains though, this can be quite difficult. There are many times in your story where you may not even see a path. You cannot see anything in the dark. Darkness, in whatever form it may take, is real. You must cling to your faith, to hope, and to love. Your hope and love may take different forms in your story. They may be your family, your friends, your purpose, your calling, your passion, your gift, or your promise. Whatever form they take in your story, you must cling to them. I decided a long time ago that if Jesus was going to use His spit and some dirt to make a blind man see, He would use anything to guide me on my journey and remind me that He is always near.

The song builds, and the bridge has the astronauts lost in space and out of contact with mission control. Suddenly, the guitar swells, the drums build, and the astronauts reconnect with mission control. They exit the eclipse and see the glorious sunlight. In a perfect twist, the artists compare this moment to finding Jesus. The light we all seek is wrapped up in Jesus. He is the Light of the World, and He should always stay as the Light of our world and stories as well.

You may believe your story so far is nothing like Noah's. You may believe that Noah completed some epic journey and your story pales in comparison. You may forget that the same Author of your story is the same God who called to Noah. Noah should stand out as someone who loved the Lord and obeyed Him at all costs. He should stand out as someone who was completely led by his faith and his desire to believe God's Word and promises. He was not a superhero. Noah was a guy who believed God had more to add to his story. Noah believed God had more to offer the world than what he saw around him every day. Like Peter, Noah listened when God said, "Follow Me." Instead of focusing on being like a certain person or feeling inadequate because you are not like your coworker or friend, commit to simply following Jesus. When He speaks, follow and obey. Let Him lead. Let Him drive. Let your faith always go before you and lead your decisions and choices. Your faith always leads to daylight. Your faith will always bring you back to your Creator. This is the key to anyone's story.

Noah's story led him to daylight and a deeper faith and hope in his Creator. One day, probably right as Noah was getting ready to mark another notch into the side of the elephant pen, the boat stopped. Now, I'm all for "mountain top" experiences, but this brought that thought to an entirely new level. The ark literally came to rest on top of a mountain! Imagine the view! I can see Noah cautiously walking out on the top deck and looking around. All he could see, for literally hundreds of miles, was water. As excited as Noah must have been to finally stop sailing, he had to realize his story was far from over. Fear still existed. Doubt must have clawed at everything inside of him. Did anyone ever question how Noah got all of the animals down off the mountain? Trust me, Noah must have had this thought!

God does this a lot. Sometimes we think He brings us to a point and wants our story to stop. Many times, this is only the beginning of our story. We can never know with full certainty what God is up to. He does not view our story in light of "beginnings" and "endings." God is constantly at work in all of it. Many times, we may stop short of what God is calling us to do. Never underestimate the work God wants to do in us and through us.

My favorite word in the Bible is "love." The Bible tells us God is love (I John 4:16). Jesus tells us all of the commandments are wrapped up in the truth that we should love God with all we have and all we are, and that we should love all other people as much as we love ourselves (Matthew 22:37-39). My second favorite word is "Jesus." There truly is power in that name! I never get tired of hearing the stories about Jesus. Whenever I read or hear or see His name, I picture Him. A lot of times He is smiling. He is always loving me. Most of the time, He is calling me. Jesus centers us. I tell people all of the time that one of my biggest prayers is for balance. Jesus is the balance. Whatever issue or struggle I am going through, He just stands on the other end (or maybe He just leans on it, or puts a hand down on it), and everything suddenly balances out.

We must get our balance right. Think about Noah. If our boat is resting at the top of a mountain, balance becomes very important. There are few things that will knock our story off track quicker than being out of balance. For me, this often means focusing on the right things and fighting the right battles! God could have called Noah to do anything. He asked him to build a giant boat. Noah had to focus on this task with everything inside of him. He was committed at every level. This was the battle God had prepared Noah to fight. He did not give Noah great strength, like Samson, to destroy his neighbors. He did not make him great with a slingshot, like David. He did not give him a dynamic evangelical preaching ability, like Billy Graham. He gave Noah great inner strength to ignore the jeers, and probably threats, and stay focused completely on getting this piece of his story exactly right.

Noah held fast to the command God had given him. It carried him through the entire ride of this part of his story, from the cutting of the first board, to the unloading of the last animal. If we have faith to take the ride, we must trust every step or wave in our journey. It does not matter what comes next; we accept it and embrace it. The best part is that sometimes the end of one ride is simply the beginning of an even better one. This is absolutely true with our own stories. Noah survived the days and nights, the animals, the fear, and every struggle. Then, his next ride and journey began. He was the one called to restart mankind. For a moment, Noah probably thought the greatest and grandest part of his story was behind him. I wonder when the next challenge hit him. Was it after the last animal was unloaded, once the boat came to rest, or during one of the restless nights? We never know when God will give us the vision for the next ride and the next season of our stories. We must simply embrace each ride, every single one, and see it all the way through. We really cannot worry about much else, or we may forget to enjoy the ride we are on. Noah had to move on and get started with the next season of his story. The previous ride was over, and there was nothing left to do but begin again. Obviously, since we are all still here, Noah succeeded. There is a small part of me though that wonders what happened to the unicorn.

WHOSE STORY IS IT ANYWAY?

There is a TV show I really enjoy called *Whose Line Is It Anyway?* It has gotten quite suggestive over the years, so I am not encouraging you to fall in love with the show, but it has a unique entertainment value because everything is completely unscripted and ad-lib. The host throws out a topic or scenario, and four actors jump in to play various roles and do outlandish things. I enjoy it most because the actors have to be creative and think on the fly, which is usually the exact opposite of how we live our lives.

Controlling Your Story

Be honest. Almost everyone likes a scripted life. I bet each of us could name five things that we you do every (or almost every) morning, and at least five more that we do in the evenings. We like order, consistency, structure, and security. These make us feel in control of our lives and give us a certain feeling of power. Here is the complete truth: it is all an illusion.

Max Lucado's book, *Anxious for Nothing*, recently challenged me at a core level. My summary of the book is you have to decide if you are going to try to control everything or if you accept the fact you control nothing. We frustrate ourselves because we fight to stay in the middle. This is not the balance we are striving for each day. This is more of a tug of war, and it will leave us completely exhausted. We know we cannot control much in our lives, but we fight and struggle to control anything we can.

TAKE A MOMENT AND LIST THE THINGS YOU ATTEMPT
TO CONTROL ON A DAILY BASIS. BE HONEST.

- _____
- _____
- _____
- _____
- _____
- _____
- _____

I'm horrible at trying to control that which is completely out of my control. Full confession—I am an extremely impatient driver. I do not drive 25 mph over the speed limit, weave in and out of traffic, and tell other drivers they are "Number 1" out the window. I only occasionally do what a lady in my church calls, "horn cussing," which is when I blow the horn instead of saying what I am thinking. I play a different game when I drive. I talk to the other drivers and tell them what they need to do. I make gentle gestures or get just close enough for someone to know I need them to drive a little differently. The problem is that they can't hear me talking or fussing. It only drives my wife completely crazy because she is the one who has to hear me!

I know the other drivers cannot hear me, but my desire to control their actions causes this rational thought to completely leave my mind when I get behind a wheel. I justify it by thinking I'm helping them to do better! It is a completely ridiculous cycle, but I get caught in it all the time. You may not struggle in this area, but I promise you there is something similar happening in your life right now. If you do struggle in this area, say a prayer for me, and I'll pray for you as well.

We all try to control our stories way more than we should. We try to control our spouses' behavior. We take it so personally when our kids say something they shouldn't and immediately act to take back control over their words and actions. We try to control our coworkers' and friends' opinions. We plan our lives perfectly and get upset when the job promotion, vacation, bonus check, social invite, or next step in our family life does not work out exactly as we had planned. We eat certain foods, work out religiously, or avoid something altogether, because we tell ourselves our health is completely in our control.

The truth is that we are all one random lightning strike, wrong-way driver, medical diagnosis, or chance encounter away from our lives changing completely. There is very little we can actually do about it, which can be either scary or exciting. We can spend every day and night worrying about something happening, or we can understand that God, who designed and created the universe down to the tiny sparrow and the smallest detail, is the Author of every moment of our stories.

Do you understand what this means for you? This is the same God who keeps the Earth in perfect orbit around the sun; designed every one of the millions of stars; created the blue whale, roses, and every part of Mount Everest; and knows and created you. He knows you intimately and completely. He formed your inmost parts and knit every cell of your body together. He knows the numbers of hairs on your head and the number of beats of your heart. He not only knows you intimately, He knows your story intimately.

God is the God of details. Have you ever studied human anatomy? The intricate layers of muscle tissue, blood vessels, and organs working in perfect unison is wondrous. He gives you a specific and exact skin tone, eye color, hair color, and pattern of skin cells that is so unique, no one else among the 7.8 billion people on Earth has this pattern on the tips of their fingers. Look at the tiny grains that make up a head of wheat, the unique design of every single snowflake, and the pattern of camouflage on the back of a baby deer, and declare that God is not concerned with detail. He is also very interested in every detail of the story of your life.

God is not simply interested in these details; He already knows them. God knows every detail of your story because He already wrote it. This is the exciting and freeing part designed to combat worry and anxiety. The God of the entire universe knows, cares, believes, and blesses your story. He sees value in every single season, in every moment, and in every single detail of your story. He gave you a story; He never intended for you to settle for a sign.

From the very beginning, God created Adam and Eve free of signs and free to live their own stories. He did not have them worry about clothes, competition, or carrying anything extra. God alone supplied their every need. It was the perfect picture of a heavenly Father caring for His children. In the garden of Eden, there was life and there was freedom.

God extended freedom to Adam and Eve because he wanted them to live for their designed purpose. They were free to love and give. They were free to hope and share relationships. Adam and Eve were free to be themselves and to live their stories. Sin entered the world. The knowledge of good and evil entered their minds and hearts (Genesis 3:1-13). All of a sudden, worry, doubt, fear, and the feeling of losing control begin to take over. Freedom to live their stories took a back seat. The baggage of worry, power, influence, fear, and anxiety became fashioned signs that simply slowed them down. Freedom calls us all to throw off these weights and live your story boldly.

The greatest gift God has provided for us is freedom. We are bound only by our own limitations, doubts, fears, and worries. God decided from the very beginning that love should be a choice. We are free to love and embrace whomever and whatever we choose. God also decided life should be a choice. In the movie *Braveheart*, William Wallace said, "Every man dies, not every man truly lives." The freedom to truly live your life is a choice you must make for yourself.

Joshua challenged God's chosen people to decide if they really wanted to live, both with boldness and with true freedom. There was slavery in Egypt or freedom in a land that waits ahead. It all seemed so simple until doubt and dread, hunger and hopelessness, and fear and frustration begin to take hold in their hearts and minds. These signs became heavy weights for the Israelites. Wandering in the wilderness, scared and weighted down, the Israelites turned back and forth towards and away from God so often, it is a wonder most of them did not die from a broken neck! Moses offered a God-designed Promised Land, tried to lead them, became angry with them, pleaded with them, and rationalized with them for years, forty to be exact. Joshua was called to finish the job. He gave them a simple choice. Choose this day, what you will do (Joshua 24:1-15).

It is a very straightforward choice. You can choose life, or you can choose death. You can choose prosperity and blessing, or disaster and calamity. You can choose to listen to and follow God, or you can choose to keep living in circles and following your own path. You can choose to keep God's commandments and walk in His ways, or you can make up your own rules.

God gives you the freedom to choose Him and the freedom to choose life. He gave you physical life, but God is talking about real life, life being lived to the fullest. Do you really think God, who spent all that time and detail creating the whole world, knitting you together just as He wanted you to be created, and designing and detailing a wondrous story orchestrated for you to live, wants you to sit there with your signs? You were designed for this moment in history. God has surrounded you with the exact people in your life that He wants you to impact. He placed you in the middle of His grand story with purpose and intent. It was not by accident or chance.

Have you ever really wondered what it took for you to come into existence? What if my grandfather didn't survive that day in 1944, fighting for his life in the Pacific Ocean? Let's extend it a little further down the line. My grandmother was ready to become engaged to another man, when my grandfather started writing her again from his hospital bed. What if his recovery had been slower, the boat back from the Pacific would have taken an extra two weeks to arrive, or the first few letters had gotten lost in the mail? Would my grandmother have waited much longer before putting my grandfather out of her mind? What if my grandfather would not have been the kindest, calmest, and most gentle and loving man when he finally returned home and swept my grandmother off her feet?

What if my mom had been a boy? My mom had terrible asthma as a child and could have died many times. Before my dad and mom got engaged, they were actually breaking up. The only thing that saved their relationship was my mom having a terrible car accident that caused my dad to rush back to her side. My mom and dad met in Morehead City, because she accepted a last-minute teaching offer and he enlisted six months early in the Coast Guard.

My dad was an alcoholic. My mom was determined to stay with him and give him grace and every opportunity to change. What if she would have walked out the door and thrown her hands up before my brother and I were born? I'm sure she had lots of reasons and plenty of opportunities.

These are just a very few of the moments which led to my story. If I really knew all that it took for me to get here, I imagine I could not even count the times and scenarios God had to work out to bring me into existence. Your story is the same. Before your story ever began, God was laying out the detailed plan required to bring you, and your story, to life. He put an unbelievable amount of time into your story before you were even the slightest gleam in your parents' eyes. He has continued to put this same love and care into your story every day since. How can we waste this glorious opportunity!

What had to happen for you to even exist and be here today?

Before God offered you the choice of life or death, the choice to accept His love and love others with the same love, He was working on your story. He did all of this to allow you the freedom to follow and embrace your story. If you are to turn your signs into a story, you must understand that your story was God's before He ever gave it to you. He cares more about your story than you do! It is almost impossible to imagine, but it is true.

Think about someone you love, truly and deeply. It could be your spouse, your kid, a brother or sister, or dear friend. Because you love them, you care deeply about their story. In many ways, their story becomes a part of your own story. Their wins in life, their accomplishments, their struggles and abilities to overcome are all celebrations for you. Their story matters to you for the simple fact that you love them.

God is the very definition of love. He loves you completely and deeply in ways you cannot even imagine. With this knowledge, how could you ever doubt He not only took the time to design your story, but cares deeply about every piece of it? Your life is an extension of God's story. It is your own. You are free to live it and make any choice that you choose. God's design, however, is to weave your story into the most wonderful tapestry of His story of love, redemption, grace, forgiveness, overcoming, and joy. Your story is connected. Your story is bigger than you ever imagined.

Connecting Your Story

Think about how many people you have met in your life. I'm sure I have met over a hundred thousand people so far in my lifetime. It actually is sort of a running joke when I go out to eat with my family, friends, or work team that I am going to see at least one other person I know in the restaurant. It used to drive my wife crazy. Now she just expects it, and knows I'm going to go over and speak for a few moments. I love people and love connecting with others. It is a huge part of my story.

Connecting with others is a huge part of your story too. I'm not just speaking to extroverts, but to all introverts and middle-of-the-roaders as well. God created us to be relational beings. One of the first thoughts we heard from God was His realization that it was not good for man to live life alone. Adam's story and Eve's story were always going to be connected.

Your story is always going to be connected to others. You must never take this for granted and must embrace every opportunity to connect and stay connected. It is a huge piece of what shapes your story and makes it better. Think about one of your better stories. It probably involves at least one other person, but most likely a group of people. The best stories come from your connections and your relationships with others.

Your story carries responsibility, because it is connected to so much more than just yourself. It is connected to your Creator. I have a sign in my garage that says, "Who you are is God's gift to you; who you become is your gift to God." It sounds cliché, but there is a lot of truth there too. If you will stop to process what God has put into your story from the very beginning, you will see God, our Creator, made a masterpiece when He created you.

The Bible actually calls us God's masterpiece (Ephesians 2:10 NIV); we are His grand design. From the very beginning of time, God really did save the best for last. On the sixth day, after making all the beauty the world contains, from the most gorgeous ocean sunset to the most magnificent creatures and the stars which illuminate the dark, He made mankind. Then, and only then, did He rest. And He rested knowing and believing it was good (Genesis 1:31).

Michelangelo did not paint the Sistine Chapel for someone to scribble over it with marker. Henry Ford never envisioned the Model T to sit still. The Wright brothers invented a flying machine so people could soar higher and go farther, not roll along and stay on the ground. In the same way, God created you to shine and soar. He created you to live a beautiful, bold story built on faith, hope, and love. You are wasting God's best creation if you choose not to embrace your story and live it boldly while staying connected to the people God has surrounded you with every day.

Creating Your Story

The story is now yours. God has given it over to you. He has provided you freedom and faith. He has given you gifts and talents to use each day. He has surrounded you with people with whom to share your story. He has created an extraordinary framework of how your life can build and become greater than you think is possible. It is now yours. God has trusted you with your story.

HOW DOES THIS MAKE YOU FEEL? WRITE DOWN
YOUR FEELINGS IN THIS MOMENT.

○ _____

○ _____

○ _____

○ _____

○ _____

○ _____

○ _____

If you did not write down scared, go back and add it to your list. Mark Batterson shares the ideas that if your dreams and prayers don't scare you, they aren't big enough for God! When I really stop and think about what God could do through my story, it is equal parts excitement and wonder mixed with fear and unworthiness.

We must give ourselves permission to wonder and imagine what God can do with our lives. We should also give ourselves permission to expect God's best. We should expect God to show up in every single circumstance and situation. He is constantly there to remind us to leave our signs behind and live our stories with beauty and boldness, even though we live in a fallen and sinful world. There is a spiritual fight between angels and demons happening all around us every single moment in every day. God is going to keep showing up in every situation, whether created by Him or not, because God is never going to leave us. If this does not fill our hearts and souls with excitement, I don't know what will fill them!

God fulfills every single piece of the word "constant," described as "occurring continuously over a period of time." If you think about God "occurring", it is a constant process of God showing up. The word "continuously" describes the very nature of who God is in His purest form. He never changes. He is and will always be God. He is going to be the most constant, continual, and forever thing you could ever try to imagine. "Over a period of time" is a reminder that He is always at work. God's timing and understanding of time is so different from mine. Yet, His timing is always perfect. It is always right. He created time, so I have complete faith He understands it at a far greater level than I ever will.

Let God stay in the center and go before you. How can God do this? He does it because He is God. The Bible is full of stories where God literally went before someone or a group of people. This happened quite often in the Old Testament. God went before Moses and the Israelite nation, both day and night. One of the absolute greatest parts was that He actually changed to fit exactly what the people needed most. In the daylight, God was a cloud. They were leaving a desert and walking to a promised land. I have spent very little time in the desert, but I would guess a cloud to cover the relentless heat of the sun beating down on my every step would probably answer my greatest prayer in those moments. At night, God was a fire. He literally would light the way, so the people could see any potential dangers. I'm simply guessing on these, but I would not want to run into any snakes, quicksand, animals who might try to eat me, or even people who might try to kill me. He was their Light, illuminating each step of the journey and each step of their story (Exodus 13:21).

God went before them again, in showing Caleb and a chosen few the actual Promised Land He prepared for them to inhabit (Numbers 13:26-30). He went before them to loosen a few bricks around the walls of Jericho so they would fall on the seventh day, just like He said would happen (Joshua 6:1-21). He went ahead and created a safe place in the midst of a raging fire to hide Shadrach, Meshach, and Abednego (Daniel 3:8-25). He called a giant fish over from across the sea, just so it would be close to the boat when Jonah was thrown overboard (Jonah 1:17). He showed up time and time again in every story because He was already there.

He also walked with them though their trials and journeys, leading them step by step. This happens all the time. God goes before you, but also stays near you always. The Bible says to draw near to God as He draws near to you (James 4:8). There are so many times you look to see where God is working and to see His hand on your story. It is vital to remember He covers it all. There are not certain times where God steps in. He is always in every detail of your story.

Your story is yours to live, but know you will never live it alone. This is the key to completing the turn from the signs that used to define you, to being ready to live your story. I hope that you have put the signs behind you, but we all know they like to sneak back up on us. Here is where I hope you will settle it once and for all. Signs are based on you and you alone. The signs you created, collected, or chose to carry were a choice made by you. God did not give them to you. God never looks at you through the lens of a sign. He will never give you a sign. He will only give you a story! Your story is based on what God has already prepared for you. Your story is based on you and God. It always has been and it always will be. When speaking about connecting and creating a story, you must understand that you are always connected to God, because He stays.

In case you ever doubt it, God has a vested interest in your story. He created it; He absolutely wants it to work! There is a lie floating around stating that God is against you. There is this thought that you are better off on your own and able to do anything you wish if you simply have enough fortitude, toughness, and willpower. That's like saying I can play basketball as good as Michael Jordan if I just work hard enough!

The truth is that one can accomplish a lot on one's own. I can work very hard at being the best at something. I could practice basketball for four hours every day, eat healthy, train my body, and study all the game film of the NBA greats. I would be a really good basketball player. After all, Spud Webb and Muggsy Bogues were extremely short by NBA standards but still succeeded at the highest level. They both were very quick, could jump extremely high (Spud Webb won an NBA dunk contest), and moved as fast with a basketball as without one. There is absolutely no way that as a stocky, 5 foot 5 ½ inch man who is limited with his vertical jump, I could make it on an NBA roster. If by some perfect balance of the universe I did perfect my shot enough to make 90% of them, I would still get blocked a ton! I would struggle to play defense, couldn't out jump anyone for rebounds, and even if I knew a player's tendencies very well, I doubt I would have the quickness to keep up with them. If I did make a roster because a general manager lost a bet, I would never see any playing time, and absolutely never be like Mike.

I could train and make myself into a really good basketball player, but my story is not the same story as Michael Jordan's. This is where so many of us fall into the trap. We work hard and have some success, but we are not living our stories! We are trying to create and write stories which were never made for us. I would spend so much time trying to be like Mike, I would never be myself. I would waste my time, my God-given gifts and talents, my relationships, and the opportunities in front of me to try to be something I was not designed to become. This is essential for us to guard against. There are people who will say that they have accomplished much in life on their own. I would argue that they have missed out on much more than they have ever accomplished. Your story is a story about you and what the Creator of the universe has prepared for you.

I love C.S. Lewis. He was one of the most brilliant and creative minds of the twentieth century. Even though he always had a brilliant, intelligent, and creative mind, his story truly turned into what it was designed to be when he accepted his story in Jesus. This is what he tried to accomplish in writing *The Chronicles of Narnia*. In his classic, *The Lion, the Witch, and the Wardrobe*, Lewis allows us to explore the real stories of Peter, Susan, Edmond, and Lucy. They were living a fairly normal life in war-time England when they were sent to live with their uncle. At his home, they stepped through the wardrobe and into the land of Narnia. Only in Narnia could they accept their rightful place and story as princes and princesses of that kingdom. They discovered who they were when they listened to Aslan, the great ruler of the land. Aslan, of course, represents Jesus. Once they followed Aslan, he showed them what they were truly created for and set their real story in motion. If they had not followed him and did not have the faith to step through the wardrobe in the first place, their story would have looked very different. Perhaps they would have been successful on the other side of the wardrobe, but they would never have been the leaders and world-changers they were designed to become in Narnia.

The Bible very clearly states we all have certain gifts and talents (Romans 12:6). We are absolutely called to use them. Jesus told a really crazy story about a man who had something his master gave him, but he didn't really know what to do with it. The servant was scared of wasting it, so he just buried it. When the master returned, he was really mad. He questioned the servant and told him, that he could have done something and put it to use in some capacity, at the very least. Jesus said the master took it from the servant completely and gave it to someone else who had proven he knew what to do with what the master had given him (Matthew 25). It sounds harsh. The truth remains that we have been given much. We absolutely must use what we have been given to live our story. If not, we waste it for ourselves and for others, and miss our purpose completely.

What gifts or talents do you have? What are you good at doing? What fuels your heart and soul? I love working with kids and have a gift in this area. My wife is amazing with the elderly. She gets them completely. She knows their needs, tendencies, and thought process. The other people she understands well are caregivers. Her discernment with both groups allows her to serve both the elderly and their caregivers in amazing ways. The resources and support she is able to provide are outstanding. There have been so many lives impacted for the better because she has used this gift and these talents in so many extraordinary ways. Individuals from her old job used to get mad because people would call and refuse to speak with anyone but her! She is living her story by serving the elderly and caregiver community. It is beautiful to witness.

Many of us get caught in the trap of truly being good at something but feeling inadequate about our gifts. We often believe we must be the best at something to make a real difference. Just because you love music and singing and feel you have a gift in this area, does not mean you must win American Idol to validate this gift. Are you good at teaching music to kids? Can you serve your church or community through singing? Do you sing to your children, family, or others to spread joy, peace, and love? Can you write music or work alongside others to create something beautiful?

I have a dear friend who is an amazing singer. However, she will tell you that she will only sing for Jesus. She sings at weddings and funerals, and for her church praise team. Her other job is being the most amazing teacher of young children. God gave her some really great musical talents, but He also gave her the unique ability to love, understand, and teach kids like no one else. She teaches the tough kids, the struggling students, those who need love desperately, and every kid who walks through her door. She teaches and reaches them all. I've never asked her if she wanted to be a professional singer. I do not know if she could have succeeded in that arena or not. What I do know is there have literally been hundreds of kids whose lives have been changed forever because she was their teacher. She let God lead her story, and she was open and willing to use her gifts to teach. She still sings and uses this gift as well, but has allowed God to balance and lead her story to make maximum impact.

WHAT ARE YOUR GIFTS AND TALENTS? WHAT HAS GOD GIVEN
YOU THE ABILITY TO DO? HOW CAN HE USE THIS TO HELP
YOU BALANCE AND LIVE YOUR STORY? WRITE THEM DOWN.

○ _____

○ _____

○ _____

○ _____

○ _____

○ _____

○ _____

You may have heard it stated, "God wants your availability, not your abilities." The truth is that God has already written your story and knows your abilities! He wants your availability so He can use those abilities. Your abilities can never be your sign. They are so much more. They will be used in a wide variety of ways to live your story. You don't hold up your "Creative" sign and just stand there. You allow God to use your creativity in your story any way He sees fit. The same is true for your "Musician" sign, your "Good with Numbers" sign, or your "Writer" sign. I have always loved to write, but God can use this gift in my story whether I am writing this book, a quick Facebook devotional, or a note of encouragement to a friend. It is important to know your gifts and talents, but it is more important to allow God to use them in any way He chooses.

The band Switchfoot is one of my favorites. They write a lot of songs about life, about keeping our priorities straight, and about living this life to the fullest. One of my favorite songs is "Meant to Live." The song challenges us to dig deep and find that purpose in our lives and to not lose ourselves in this process. This is a dynamic challenge and at the core of moving completely past your signs, embracing your gifts and talents, and living your story the way God designed. If you have ever wondered if this is all there is to this life, you are awakening to your God-ordained story. If you have ever thought you could do more and make a bigger or better difference in this world, God is stirring in your soul. God is calling you back to Him. God is preparing you for more. God is tired of you being content with what this world has to offer. Your story, your gifts, and your future is so much greater than you can imagine.

SECTION 3

EMBRACE YOUR STORY

Your story was designed by God with great care and love. As much as He loves you, He loves your story, your gifts, and your potential equally. They are all a part of your design and your story! What can you do to fall more deeply in love with your story? You have a great story, composed by the Creator, and that it is waiting to be lived boldly by you. Your story is worth falling in love with and embracing. Where there is love, there is always an embrace.

I have been blessed to perform almost a dozen weddings. My favorite part of any wedding is the final act. The look on the groom's face right before you tell him he may now "kiss your bride" is like no other. The newly married couple embraces, but it is so much greater than the physical embrace. This embrace is the affirmation of all that has been and the belief that greater things await. It is a culmination of all that has led to this point and all that is promised to come. The embrace also fully solidifies the commitment, the promise, and the vows.

Embrace your story in this manner. Make the commitment to your story, believe the promise that God has written you a grand story to live, and make the vow to yourself that your story is valuable beyond measure. What is still holding you back from fully embracing your story? Sometimes it is easier to make the excuses than to actually make the choice to live your story.

Today, you leave behind the signs, and you believe in your story. Today, you decide to not be defined by one characteristic, one moment from the past, or one mistake. Today, you embrace your story of love and hope, and cling to courage and faith. You choose to take the ride and the risks. Today, you know God has not only gone before you to write a grand story for you, but He is walking with you every step of the way. Today, I pray, you live this life to the fullest.

EMBRACE TODAY

Your story does not start today. Your story started way before the day you were born. Do not believe the lie that your story starts from this moment. We have already discussed how God will use your past and all parts of your story to shape you. He has brought you to this point and to this day, and He wants you to hear His voice and follow His lead.

There are few things that soothe the soul like the voice of someone you love and care about. It can be the voice of a spouse, parent, sibling, child, or close friend. When they speak, it soothes the deepest parts of your soul. You listen to the words, but most importantly, you hear the care, love, and connection pour through their voice. I love hearing my wife's voice when she calls just to tell me hello. I love hearing her voice at night right before she goes to sleep. I love hearing her laugh and when she gets excited about something. I also love hearing the voices of my kids. Their laughter, excitement, frustration, and questions all have certain tones and flows. I know their voices. They can call out "Dad" in the middle of a crowded street, and I still hear them. There is a connection far deeper than just the words or their voices.

I love hearing the voice of my brother. We're identical twins and sound very much alike. Since we are twins, and he has known me longer than anyone, I love hearing his voice because I know he "gets" me. If I am excited, frustrated, annoyed, or overjoyed, he is going to get it. It is not just because we often think alike and are driven by similar interests and passions; the feeling is deeper. It is a connection I can always count on. Think about the voice that speaks the loudest to your heart. God is speaking to your heart too. He is connecting with you at the deepest level. He "gets" you and wants you to know this truth completely. He is speaking about your story. He is speaking about your worth. He is calling you deeper into the water and farther away from the security of the shore.

Accept Your Story

Your story may take you farther than you ever thought you would go. I wanted to play football in college. I was actually a pretty good football player and made the all-conference and all-county teams my senior year. There was one big problem when I went for a recruiting visit—I was always shorter than the recruiter. However, I refused to let my "Short" sign define me. I visited one college close to home but had to travel for the rest. Apparently, there was a greater need for shorter football players outside the state of North Carolina.

My mom and I took a trip to Kentucky to visit a college, and I went down to South Carolina as well. There was also a college in Tennessee. I had actually never set foot in Tennessee before this visit. For the first time, I was actually realizing my life, my steps, and my story were needing a little more guidance than just my own head and my heart. God was working in my spirit and opening my eyes to see Him developing my story. I had been praying for an opportunity to play football and was not going to let "where" I was going to play stop me. So, for the first time in my life, I set my feet down in Tennessee and went to a little Division III school outside of Knoxville, called Maryville College.

God may ask you to go somewhere you have never been before. He may ask you to travel out of your comfort zone and away from what you know. He may do this to build your faith in incredible ways and to bring you to a place where you know absolutely no one. When it's just you and the Lord, you come to realize, for this part, and really any part of your story, He is all that you need.

I would not have traded one moment of my time in Tennessee. In fact, it was during this period that God started showing me there was much more to my story than I had ever realized.

Have you come to that point? Think back to a moment or certain moments of your time on this earth when you have realized your story may be bigger than you first thought.

WRITE THEM DOWN. THESE ARE IMPORTANT MOMENTS
TO COME BACK TO WHEN YOU DOUBT YOUR STORY.

o _____

o _____

o _____

o _____

o _____

o _____

o _____

Your story only gets bigger and larger when you pour into it. The more you understand you have a story to live that may increase your current boundaries and expectations, the greater the possibilities of what that story may become. If you are not actively living and seeking your story, it will never grow like God intended. By walking your story daily in faith, you will see it grow and take shape.

When I worked as a children's pastor, I had the amazing privilege (twice actually) of hosting the Strength Team at our church. If you have never heard of or watched these guys, you are really missing out. The way I would always describe them to others is, "You know the guys that smash a wall of bricks, bend steel pipes, snap baseball bats, and tell people about Jesus." These guys were everything you would imagine they would be, including being fairly massive.

One of our local restaurants agreed to serve them food each day of their stay. They went to the restaurant for breakfast and lunch, and the owner assured us that they could eat as much as they wanted or needed. This was almost twelve years ago, but I still remember some of the meals like they were yesterday. I can eat, but these guys ate! One of the members asked for an omelet made of twelve eggs and every type of breakfast meat on the menu! He ate it all. Another one of the guys really enjoyed liver mush. He ate seven helpings before he actually ate his breakfast. I won't even go into describing what happened at lunch.

If these guys were going to be able to work out for hours a day and hone their craft of destroying very strong objects, they had to fuel their bodies in preparation. The stories of our lives must be the same. They must be fueled to grow. We must put more faith, more hope, and more love into our stories. We must strengthen and grow them by the manner in which we live our lives. If we shrink back from our stories, they will never grow as large and magnificent as God has intended. We must feed and fuel our stories by refusing to step backwards and put our signs back on. We feed our stories by taking risks in faith and listening to where God is leading our hearts and spirits. We feed them when we give, love, hope, persevere, care, and embrace where God is moving and working. If we feed our stories in preparation for where God is leading, we will have all we need when we get there.

The story of Elijah, one of God's great prophets, gives us a deeper insight into this example. Elijah was God's chosen man. God wrote his story as one of the greatest prophets in the history of the Israelite nation and the world. He was given all the gifts he needed to call people back to God. God had written his story and knew about his great accomplishments, lowest moments, and final victory before any of it was realized by Elijah himself.

Elijah's greatest triumph was going toe-to-toe with the prophets of Baal. These prophets of Baal had all the fame and notoriety of the day. They were cocky, boastful, and arrogant. They did horrible things in the name of their god. One day, a new challenger stepped into the ring. Elijah wasn't much to look at, and these prophets certainly did not seem afraid. But Elijah had a fire building inside of him that was unmatched. It had been fanned by the living God who kept showing Himself to be faithful and true. Elijah had learned to trust Him, to walk in His truths, and to know that the power of God was greater than any power on earth. His fire was going to come out at the perfect time.

The prophets of Baal created an elaborate stage show. Interestingly enough, they wanted fire to be their measuring stick. They built a fancy altar and challenged Elijah to a contest. Whichever "god," be it Baal or the God of Elijah, could send fire from heaven to burn the offering would be the one true God. This was a literal life-or-death showdown that would make Ali vs. Frazier look like a small-time circus act.

The prophets of Baal started first. They called and danced and yelled and pleaded with their god. When this did not work, they turned to more extreme measures. They cut their bodies and let their own blood pour on the altar. They amped up the antics and put on a show that I feel confident would have been heard for miles. Elijah was not deterred (1 Kings 18).

How could Elijah live this part of his story with such boldness? He was outnumbered 450 to 1! He knew the reputations of these guys, and they intended to win at all cost. His very life was at stake. Yet, he stood there, jeering at them. His confidence was greater than anything they could throw at him. God had been preparing Elijah for this exact moment. Elijah had been spending time with God in prayer. He had been listening to God and learning from Him. The fire growing inside of him was nothing compared to the fire God would bring down upon these false prophets of Baal.

Elijah patiently waited his turn. When these other men could do nothing more and had exhausted themselves completely, Elijah took center stage. Before he proved the power of his God, he wanted to make sure these false prophets understood God's power and saw His might clearly. He doused the offering with water and filled up a trench around the altar with flowing water. Then, he looked up to heaven and prayed. Elijah knew God would answer his prayer and prove that He was the God of everything.

There are times you simply must live your story boldly. There are times you must trust God completely. Sometimes, these two moments intersect. This is what happened with Elijah. God sent down a fire so amazing that it lapped up the water and burned the offering and the entire altar completely. It was a message sent loud and clear. Elijah killed the prophets and stood victorious with the Lord. Elijah had lived his story fully, and God was glorified wholly and completely.

If you've never heard the story before, you would expect the happy ending to wrap it all up. Only, the happy ending for Elijah's story came later. Not long thereafter, Elijah completely forgot his story and grabbed hold of his sign, which was actually a "Wanted" poster. His sign said "Scared" or "Afraid." Jezebel, the great wicked queen of the region, heard this news about the destruction of the prophets. She immediately set out to capture and kill Elijah. The same bold Elijah who mocked his adversaries and that God used to call down the very fire from Heaven, would have definitely won an Oscar for his portrayal of the Cowardly Lion.

Elijah became scared and distraught. He told God that he would rather die than live in this fear and uncertainty. The same guy who had shown such courage and confidence was shrinking back from his story and giving up on it completely. This happens all the time in our lives as well. We want to live fearless, but our head gets in the way of our heart. We want to be bold in our actions and in our stories, but find ourselves hesitating, doubting, and questioning.

WHAT OFTEN DISTRACTS YOU, DISRUPTS YOU,
OR DISCOURAGES YOU? NAME THEM HERE AND
PRAY OVER THEM. KNOW THAT THEY ARE ONLY
PULLING YOU BACK FROM YOUR STORY.

- _____
- _____
- _____
- _____
- _____
- _____
- _____

Despite the distractions and fears, God never gave up on Elijah. Rest assured, God will never give up on you. God did some pretty amazing things to restore Elijah. He met his physical needs and his spiritual needs. God called Elijah by name (1 King 19). He connected with him and asked him, "What are you doing here, Elijah?" God was really saying to Elijah: This is not a part of your story. You are hiding. You are scared. You are holding up a sign and allowing it to define you. You are more than what you see in this moment. Let's live your story together and get back to doing what I created you to do!

This is a question we need to ask ourselves more often. This is a question we need to listen to God asking us throughout our lives. "What are you doing here, [insert name]?" There will be times in our stories when we feel completely lost. It may be because of choices we made or circumstances far beyond our control. Either way, God will be there, asking us to think about what we are really doing in that place.

You need to ask yourself this question in both the small and grand moments. If you truly wish to embrace your story, you must give God permission to ask you this same question often. There is so much power behind this question. Stop and think about what you have accomplished today. Think about the moments you would be proud for God to intervene and ask, "What are you doing here?" There are probably also moments you would be ashamed. In the past month, there have been moments you would probably proudly promote and moments you would love to erase. The key is letting God speak to your heart and being honest with Him about the moments. Let Him speak and be ready to listen.

This is a powerful question because it can be framed in so many ways. Listen to God asking you that question—in love. "What are you doing here,...?" I picture Him coming to us, picking us up, and giving us the best hug. Imagine God asking you this when you are lost. You are the lost sheep He helps out of the ravine, gently asking "What are you doing here?" You may find yourself as the prodigal son or daughter at a time in your story. It's okay. God can find you anywhere in your story, clean you up, and ask, "What are you doing here?" He will remind you that this is not what He created you for and move you back into His will and His love. Commit to doing a better job of stopping and listening to God's question. Challenge yourself to be responsive to this question as God guides your story back where or how you are designed to live.

This is the part we have come to fear the most. There are many times we fall into the same trap Elijah found, and do the same thing to our own stories. We are living them completely and fully when we suddenly get distracted, disrupted, or discouraged. This happens in thousands of different ways. It happens when someone we trust and love tells us something we don't want to hear. It may even be true, but we can't accept it. Our career path, family plan, or years of planning suddenly falls into pieces. A situation does not work out like we wanted it to, and we grab our sign, shrink back, and hide. Sometimes, we literally hide. Other times, we hide our thoughts, feelings, and vision for our future. The great news is this happens to everyone. If it can happen to the heroes of our faith from the Bible, we should expect it to happen to us.

This is where control, or at least the appearance of control, must leave. Like your signs, you must leave control at the feet of the One who controls it all. You must be willing to follow where He calls and where He leads. The same voice that spoke to Elijah in a whisper and called Peter out of the boat, is calling you into the water. Listen to the voice of Jesus. You can trust it.

You can trust the voice of Jesus because He is calling you by name. Did you ever think about why the disciples trusted Him when He first called out to them? I can't help but wonder if it wasn't because of the familiarity of the voice which called them by name. I wonder if it was a voice they had heard since they were little. Was it the same voice they heard deep down in their souls, in their hearts, or in their spirits? Was it the voice of faith and courage? Had this same voice not comforted them in times of heartache, challenged them in the times of uncertainty, and reminded them of a deep love surrounding them at all times?

Jesus knew their names. He called each disciple directly and by name. He knew them. There's a funny thing about someone calling out your name. My twin brother's name is Daniel. When we were growing up, very few people could tell us apart. By the time we were in high school, our football coach could never get our names right. It was probably the second week of practice when he announced to both of us, "I'm calling you Smitty. If I yell 'Smitty,' I need both of you to turn around!" To this day, if someone yells "Christopher", "Chris", "Daniel", or "Smitty", I'm going to turn around. I have accepted all of them as my name. Whatever name you will answer to, Jesus is calling. Take this as your roll call.

Do you remember getting called by name for the morning roll call in elementary school? It was really pointless. As an elementary principal today, I would consider this a complete waste of time. Maybe you have seen the videos of the teacher greeting their students at the door with a special handshake, fist bump, dance move, or choreographed series of high fives, daps, and greetings. Which would you want to wake you up to live your story each day?

Too many times we approach our story like the high school teacher in *Ferris Bueller's Day Off* (Bueller? Bueller?) trying to motivate us to start our day. We need to be ready to embrace each moment. We need to wake up each day and know God has our special greeting ready to go. He is ready every single day to welcome us into our story.

WHAT ARE YOUR FIRST THOUGHTS WHEN YOU WAKE UP IN THE MORNING?

○ _____

○ _____

○ _____

○ _____

○ _____

○ _____

○ _____

How you start your day is critical. I used to be so impressed with my pastor when I started in church ministry. He was almost seventy years old at the time and passionately loved his ministry, job, and people. He had a quiet energy that was always present. I remember talking with him one day at lunch when he shared that he hadn't used an alarm clock in over 40 years! He said, "The Lord wakes me up every morning and I'm ready to go." If you are someone who hits the snooze button four or more times a day, you probably think I'm lying. He had such a great attitude about his life, calling, purpose, and story, he woke up ready to live it. He expected God to wake him up with a personalized greeting and get his story started!

The end of your day matters too. So many people have trouble sleeping or falling asleep. You may need to let God ask you His question one more time at night when you are mindlessly scrolling through social media, increasing your anxiety over the nightly news, or replaying your mistakes and frustrations from the day over again through your mind. You must learn to end the day with Jesus. You lay it all back at His feet. If it was a great day, you give Him praise. If it was a terrible day, you give Him praise, and you ask for more. Whether you need more faith, more hope, more love, more patience, more laughter, more joy, more praise, or more answers, you ask Him for more. Then, you go to sleep believing you will receive what you have asked our Father to provide.

11

EMBRACE THE STRUGGLE

Our stories often times get stuck. Like Bill Murray in *Groundhog Day*, we find ourselves repeating the same actions, same patterns, same behaviors, and often the same mistakes. I grew up listening to records. There is something about the sound quality, the feel of the record, and the sound when the needle drops and the music begins. As beautiful as this sound can be, there is nothing worse than having the music engulf you and right at your favorite part, the record become stuck. The same phrase and same notes repeat over and over again. All the beauty and power simply get sucked out in that exact moment. Our lives can be the same way. Getting stuck in autopilot can be very destructive for our hearts and souls. It can suck all the joy, fulfillment, excitement, love, and purpose out of our everyday lives.

Getting stuck in a continual loop hurts us in a number of ways. It numbs our senses, therefore stealing our joy. We become comfortable with seeing less, listening less, experiencing less, enjoying less, and living less. There is this belief, like all cars designed today, we too can select cruise control as an option for our everyday lives. We wake up, press the button, and go through the motions. We have tricked ourselves into believing this works best. It does not.

I worked with a friend in high school who was passionate about only driving cars with straight drive transmissions. I still remember him telling me, if you are not able to press in the clutch and shift the manual gears, you are not really driving your car. His belief was an automatic car was simply driving you. There is a lot of truth in this analogy when we step back and take a hard, focused look at the days and moments of our lives. When we accept pressing cruise control, we accept we are not in full control of our stories. We relinquish a part of our stories back to our signs. We are missing out on our stories because we are not adding anything new. We are not taking in anything new and do not process anything new. We begin to think our stories get stuck somewhere in the middle and live on repeat.

IN WHAT AREAS OF YOUR LIFE DO YOU
FIND YOURSELF STUCK ON REPEAT?

- _____
- _____
- _____
- _____
- _____
- _____
- _____

Challenge Your Story

I was diagnosed with sleep apnea about a year ago. I've tried a couple of different masks but simply cannot get used to transforming into Darth Vader every night. Even though I was told by my doctor that I will feel better by getting more quality sleep, I choose to not wear a mask because it's "different." I also make my wife quite unhappy and get kicked out of the bed from snoring any time my allergies flair up. Why does my mind tell me this is a better alternative than simply wearing a mask I know I can learn to utilize? It's my comfort level. It's understanding that I can break a cycle that is not good for me and find a better way.

The Avett Brothers, probably my all-time favorite band, has a powerful message wrapped up in their "Salvation Song." They sing about their purpose. They remind us that even though they are just two good ol' country boys from North Carolina, they sing and live with a purpose. Ultimately, they challenge us to believe that we exist to leave behind something better and to show others a better way. Isn't this how we should live our lives, looking for better in everything?

Living our lives for the better can be hard. Our stories, no matter how grand we believe they have been written and no matter how much passion we pour into them, can be hard. When we press cruise control, we are often times allowing ourselves to relax. Think about how we press that button in our cars, and we immediately allow ourselves to relax and adjust. This is okay to a point. When we relax too much in our cars, we lose awareness and risk putting ourselves in serious danger.

Once we really relax, we embrace a lack of feeling, and we start to become numb. We numb ourselves a lot. It comes in tons of forms. There are drugs, both legal and illegal. There are addictions. These come in a menagerie of measures—everything from beer to binge watching, pornography to picture perfect, and shopping to sugars. We are addicted with all of these things, even though they tend to keep us locked into our cycles, rather than freeing us from them. Like pressing cruise control, this type of numbing slows and ignores our feelings. Most importantly, it slows and ignores our stories.

This world can come at you extremely fast. A pause button may seem like a good idea, but the same things you left at the pause will always be more complicated and piled up deeper when you return. It's like the laundry basket when you just simply get tired of doing laundry and take a week off. It's all still there, it has multiplied, and it stinks! Refuse to press pause. You must embrace your story, even in the struggle. You have too many moments you will miss.

WHAT DO YOU DO TO NUMB YOURSELF?

o _____

o _____

o _____

o _____

o _____

o _____

o _____

We press cruise control because somehow have become okay with "fine." This is a sign; "Fine" is not how to live our stories. The hard truth is that this movement into a cycle and into numbing ourselves is a slow fade. We don't wake up one day and decide to drink three beers a day for the rest of our lives. We do not intentionally plan to overeat each day for the next 675 days until we find ourselves forty pounds overweight and miserable. We don't take a job knowing for the next seventeen years, we will simply go through the motions and play the game well enough to not get fired. We don't take the first sip, first look, first thought, and envision how empty it will leave us feeling years from now. Like a small crack in the iceberg that grows over time, it builds until it often times comes crashing down. The slow fade made a big mess.

Have you ever watched a spider? I know, they are not really anyone's favorite to enjoy. Unfortunately, ever since I fell in love with *Charlotte's Web* when I was a seven-year-old at White Lake where my mom read two chapters a night on vacation, I pay attention to spiders. Charlotte allowed me to understand spiders on a deeper level. They really are quite interesting to observe.

Spiders weave their webs with skill and precision. Everything they do in regard to their webs is with purpose. Their very lives depend on the webs working well. Then, they wait. The unsuspecting victim certainly does not have death and destruction on their mind. For all we know, the little insect might be having the time of its life and living its story to the full. All of a sudden, it finds itself stuck. The poor guy doesn't even realize how bad its stuck and probably thinks this is a momentary setback. It struggles, but that only makes the situation worse. The caught insect has no idea what it is actually fighting against. It does not fight with skill and purpose; it fights aimlessly, and oftentimes, creates a completely inescapable trap for itself. The spider sees the green light. It injects the insect with poison, to numb it and dull the senses. Before long, the hopeless insect is tangled in a giant mess and completely numb to the entire situation. The day didn't start this way, and it wasn't where the insect hoped to end up. The insect did not know it's enemy, did not understand the trap, and thought it could make it out all by itself. This story does not have a happy ending.

Have you caught the correlation yet? We fall into the trap. Our stories are stuck, and our lives are stuck. It is very rare that every component of our stories and lives become a tangled mess. It is usually just one piece, but it is always an essential piece to our complete story. We often have no idea we are even stuck at first or what we are stuck up against. We may struggle, but it is rarely with purpose. The struggle is often without conviction. Sometimes, the struggle is very real, but we have just about given up hope of anything ever really changing. It certainly is a precarious position we often find ourselves in. One thing is for certain; our stories and our lives really do become stuck. It is almost impossible to turn the page to the next part of our story.

WHAT "TRAPS" DO YOU ROUTINELY FALL INTO
IN YOUR ATTEMPTS TO PRESS CRUISE CONTROL,
RELAX, OR NUMB YOURSELF TO YOUR STORY?

- _____
- _____
- _____
- _____
- _____
- _____
- _____

We struggle in our own web of doubts, lies, signs, addictions, and pains. The doubts about our stories, and our struggles with our own inadequacies, take hold. The lies we believe or have heard about ourselves become almost deafening. The signs we desperately want to abandon keep showing back up. The addictions, which started small and innocent, now consume a part of our lives. The pains that accompany a sinful world remind us every day that we are not home yet. All of these tangle, twist, and keep us from living out our stories.

Jesus met a man, one time, who had been stuck in his own web of doubt, self-pity, physical hurt, and shame for thirty-eight years. Jesus was coming back to Jerusalem to celebrate a Jewish holiday. On His way, He passed by the pool of Bethesda. This was certainly not a recreational pool or anything beautiful to behold. It was a place of sickness and sadness. There was a rumor floating around that an angel would come stir the water, and the first person to touch it would be healed completely. People laid around this pool for years; some laid there for decades. I kind of think Jesus knew who had been there the longest and who was stuck really deep in their web. Jesus sought out the guy who was frozen completely and felt utterly helpless. Knowing this man had been laying there for thirty-eight years and unable to get to the pool first because he had a disability, Jesus asked the most obvious question imaginable. He just threw it out there like a slow-pitch softball, waiting to be crushed. "Do you want to be healed?" Jesus asked (John5:6).

Jesus asks us the same question. He often does it when we are stuck in a problem or situation that we landed in or created. With Jesus, it doesn't matter. What matters is understanding that Jesus shows up in our stories. He shows up to rescue us, to restore us, and to remind us better stories are waiting.

Are you tired of being stuck? Do you want to get out of that web? Are you ready to live your story?

The interaction between Jesus and the man with a disability plays out a lot like our conversations with Jesus today.

Jesus: "Do you want some help?"

You or I: "I do, but [insert excuse after excuse]."

Jesus: "Well..."

You or I (interrupting Jesus): "But, [insert excuse after excuse]."

Jesus (who has already freed us from the web completely while we have been making excuses): "Come on out; I got you!"

You or I: "I can't believe it; I'm free!"

Do you know what has to occur if you want to be able to walk? It's actually quite simple. Stand up! Get up! Get off the floor and quit laying there. What do you think Jesus said to this man? Yep, you guessed it. Jesus looked right at him and said, "Get up, take up your bed, and walk" (John 5:8).

Do you know what you must do if you want to quit struggling in your webs of lies, signs, pains, and addictions? Jesus is telling you the exact same thing over two thousand years later! Get up! Get out! Stop struggling in vain to fight a fight you really can't win on your own anyway. You are free through the blood and grace and promises of Jesus. Stand up and walk away. Get out of the web; walk away from it. Leave the web in your past and be free to live your story. Jesus cannot say it with any more simplicity. It cannot be any more direct. Laying and waiting in worry, tossing and turning in unbelief and doubt is never the answer. Commit today to getting out of the web. It is not always easy, but Jesus came to set you free. Accept His freedom. Let His freedom pull you out and allow you to get back to living your story!

12

EMBRACE IT TOGETHER

Jesus puts people in our paths to serve as His hands and feet in our stories as well. I call these people "freedom fighters." God puts them in our paths to help show us that freedom is possible. They fight with us and for us so that we you can experience true freedom and live our stories. God created us as relational beings and many times, God will use these people to help free us as well.

Have you ever thought how simple it would be to escape a web if you had someone else holding it open for you? What if you had someone providing you encouragement to not give up? Could someone provide you direction and support so you know with much greater clarity what you are fighting against?

Ropes are a lot like webs. Have you ever been tempted to try the rope ladders at the fair or amusement parks? They seem simple enough, but the second you put a foot or hand on it, the whole rope system starts shaking. The more you try to regain your balance and stop the shaking, the more off-balance you become. The rope is so loose it vibrates and shakes to the point there is no way to hang on. You give up and fall off. It is inevitable. Do you know how easy it is to climb a rope if someone is holding it still for you? When someone holds the rope tight for you and absorbs your vibrations, climbing the rope ladder becomes very simple.

Connect Your Story

WHO ARE YOUR FREEDOM FIGHTERS? WHO
FIGHTS ALONGSIDE YOU AND FOR YOU?

- _____
- _____
- _____
- _____
- _____
- _____
- _____

We talked about the word "alongside" earlier. Having people come alongside us is powerful in our pursuit of true freedom. These are the people who believe in us and our stories, and are fully committed in helping us live every single moment. They don't want to see us stuck in our stories! They know we are destined for greater things. God always supplies these people in the moments we need them. Occasionally, we are too stubborn, blinded, or distracted to see them, but these people exist in our lives.

Being a principal is a tough job. It's a lonely job. (I heard this in grad school but did not believe it. I should have listened to my professor.) There are very few people who have the same vantage point and carry the same weight as we do on a daily basis. If we care about people and want the best for every single student, teacher, staff member, and family I serve, that's a lot to balance. No matter how much I love my job (and I love serving as a principal at my current school more than I ever thought I would love any job), there are times it puts a strain on my story.

I would have never made it ten years in this role if it were not for other people showing up in the exact moments to come alongside me. Some of them stayed for a moment, and others for a long while. I have received a powerful card with words of affirmation at the exact time I needed it. A thankful email or message from a parent came on the heels of an extremely trying day. A colleague from another school system texted at the exact right moment to help me stay focused and encouraged.

Every day of my life now, God surrounds me with two assistant principals who truly are two of the absolute greatest people in the world. They always seek opportunities to pull me out and pull me up. They refuse to let me get down or stay down. In every circumstance, I know I will never be left alone to fight the battle and struggle on my own. God allows them to be His hands and feet and voice. We laugh together, pray together, learn together, and share life together. We lead our school together with boldness and courage, conviction and care. We support every aspect of our lives, both work and home related, and walk alongside each other to live and share our stories together.

It's great to have these people in our lives. They are our freedom fighters. They remind us our stories are meant to be lived in freedom and lived to the fullest. It's also great to be a freedom fighter for others as well. Once we have experienced this power in our own lives, it is easy to live this out for others and come alongside them. Never underestimate this opportunity. We all have a part of our own stories that involves being this freedom fighter for another person. We must be ready to embrace this role and allow this part of our story to be written in bold, powerful letters.

The Gospels record a story that gives us a glimpse of four freedom fighters. One day, four friends walked into a situation and knew something needed to change. They saw the opportunity and believed they could help. They heard about this Jesus guy who was doing the impossible. Their friend needed a dose of the impossible. They knew they had to get their friend to Jesus. But, that was kind of the problem. Their friend could not go anywhere or get to Jesus because he was lame and stuck in one spot. These freedom fighters knew they had to bridge the gap between their friend and Jesus. They tossed him on a mat and each friend grabbed a corner. They started walking towards Jesus (Mark 2:1-12).

In moments where we embrace the ability to fight and stand in the gap for others, their story becomes our story. The stories are interlocked and allowed to unfold together. I don't know how far they walked and how much actual thought these friends put into their plan. I do know that when they got to Jesus, their plan looked ridiculous. Here is the pivotal moment we cannot miss in their lives or our own. With God, nothing is impossible. These friends came for a purpose and to experience what they had always been told was impossible. Their friend's sign was old. His "Lame" sign was getting to be too much. It was torn and rough, and everyone was frankly tired of seeing it. They believed their friend had a better story yet to be lived beyond this sign.

Once you have true conviction that God is ready to move in your life or in the life of someone that He has allowed to intersect with your story, "Impossible" becomes another sign you can leave behind. A great crowd blocking the way to Jesus was not going to stop their friend's story. I don't know what happened next, but before anyone knew it, the five men had somehow made it to the top of the roof, mat and all. Then, they started digging. They dug through the roof—mud, thatch, and mess. They carefully lowered their friend down to Jesus. Jesus loved their idea, and most importantly, their faith. He told the man who laid there lame on his mat that his story was about to change forever. From that point forward, Jesus said his sins and his signs were in the past. Jesus healed his heart and his soul before He even worried about the legs. Of course, many people didn't approve of all this commotion and talk of forgiveness and new life. Jesus decided to show everyone that He makes all things new and can restore all things. So, He went ahead and healed the man's legs too. Jesus started a new chapter and turned the page on the past. I feel certain that this changed the chapter and story for the four friends too. One can't be a part of a miracle and stay the same. This is simply how Jesus works in our lives and stories.

If you have been looking at your signs and story so far and refusing to look past the impossible, I pray you experience the faith to move past the thoughts of things in your life or in the life of someone close to you that once seemed impossible. Albert Einstein has a quote attributed to him stating, "There are only two ways to live your life. One is as though nothing is a miracle. The other is as though everything is a miracle." Look around and you will find the impossible in everything God has created. It is aerodynamically impossible for bumblebees to fly. Water-striding insects can literally walk on water. You and I are both here in this moment with a story to live out in its entirety. It is not only a miracle you are here; it is a miracle you are here in this moment, at this exact time. Your story was written for right now.

13

MILLIONS OF MOMENTS

Bruce Lee said it well, "The meaning of life is that it is to be *lived*." Jesus said it best. "I have come that they may have life, and have it to the full." (John 10:10 NIV) Another way the Bible conveys this message is Jesus may have said it more like this, "I have come that you may have life, a great full life." A full life is one overflowing with purpose and commitment. It is designed to be epic. The truth about making something epic is that you do not really know it is going to be epic when you start. How many people do you think wake up and expect today to be epic or extraordinary? Very few people start any project knowing it will be epic. There is no real way to know.

The opposite is true as well. Many people start out with a great, surefire idea or plan that is guaranteed not to fail. It is every "get rich quick" scheme rolled up into one. These rarely come to fruition and leave people frustrated and disappointed. They can even cause people to give up on their stories. It goes back to the idea that we want a guarantee and a promise of success. No story comes with this type of certainty. Faith requires more of our stories. Our stories do not have scripts, but they do have moments. Your story is actually made up of millions on moments.

The average life span contains approximately twenty-two million seconds. When I think about a moment, it may last for a second, or it may last for ten seconds. Either way, most of our lives will be made up of millions of moments. We must embrace them. We must cherish each and every one and deeply desire to make the most of each moment we are given. This is how our stories unfold. We do not know the future and cannot predict our own stories. We can focus on the moments provided for us today with the goal of making them extraordinary or epic.

WHAT MOMENTS DID YOU EMBRACE TODAY?
WHICH MOMENTS DO YOU REMEMBER?

o _____

o _____

o _____

o _____

o _____

o _____

o _____

Think back to when you were a little kid. The world made a lot of sense, even though almost everything was completely out of your control. Your life flowed through each moment. You played until it was time for dinner. You enjoyed the laughter and friendship, and did not worry about what was coming next. You woke up excited and approached each day with great expectation, believing it was going to be good.

What has happened to us? In our pursuit of certainty, comfort, and convenience, we have given up on the excitement and dream of being extraordinary and epic.

There is no greater example of how to embrace our stories than the story of Jesus Himself. Jesus was the Master of making the most of His moments. He calmed storms, healed the sick, raised the dead to life, and cast out demons by the thousands. He also sat with children, took time to talk and listen to people one on one, spent countless hours praying alone, and poured deeply into twelve men who He believed could help change the world. Jesus certainly lived life to the full, but His definition of "full" was much different than ours today.

Jesus never hurried. He was never early, and He was never late. He knew each moment had a purpose and lived it completely before He moved on to the next moment. Even when Mary and

Martha approached Him so confused over His timeline, Jesus was still, right on time. As Martha chastised Him and told Him, "If you had been here (on time), my brother would not have died" (John 11:21). Jesus understood her, and He understood this moment. Lazarus was dead and his sisters thought he had more of a story waiting to be lived. They were distraught and they were heartbroken. They wanted to know where Jesus was in that moment of his death and why He didn't change it. Jesus was about to show them He created that moment for a reason.

Jesus wept. He wept for the moment. He wept because He was human, with human emotions and human tears. He wept because He could feel the pain and hurt inside the people and family of Lazarus surrounding Him. These were real people weeping in despair for the loss of a loved one. He wept for Lazarus and the testimony Lazarus would be able to share with so many. Jesus also knew He was calling Lazarus back from the glory of Heaven into a sinful and struggling world. Jesus knew that moment was made for a miracle. He raised Lazarus from the dead to prove He has power over everything, even life and death (John 11:33-43).

The very same power Jesus used to raise the dead and perform every single miracle is calling you to live your moments. These moments are yours and they are meant to be lived to the full. Stop and think for a moment. Jesus knew one of Lazarus' moments was his death; He also knew one moment would be the day He would call out Lazarus' name and bring him back to life. I feel completely confident Lazarus also had "less spectacular moments," like being kind to a neighbor, meeting the need of a friend, playing games with his sisters as a child, providing an encouraging word in the right moment, and sharing a great testimony about the time he met Jesus in nothing but his burial linens.

These millions of moments in our lives are exactly what creates our stories. Some may argue that we need exciting moments and powerful moments and dynamic moments to make a great story. I would argue that if we understand the value of these moments and realize the potential of each and every one, we can create an incredible story out of the "ordinary" moments.

Think of about the word "extraordinary." It is a compound word made up of two single words. "Extra" simply means to be greater than usual. "Ordinary" means normal, commonplace, or standard. When we choose to embrace each moment of our lives and live our God-given stories, we put something extra, even in the ordinary. We choose to make the ordinary moments more epic because we realize they are creating our stories. We realize every single moment can make a difference. The power of each moment is anything but ordinary; it must be viewed as extraordinary. As we begin to understand the power of these moments, we catch a greater glimpse of what Jesus meant when He spoke about "life to the full."

In a moment, you may have fallen in love. It only took a moment for a guy to drop to one knee. It only took a moment for his future bride to say, "yes." In a moment, you accepted a job offer. In a moment, a baby let out its first cry. It only took a moment to give someone a hug who desperately needed it. It took a single moment to choose forgiveness, and another moment to offer it to another. I pray you have embraced the love of God, shown perfectly in His Son Jesus. This only took a moment as well. Most of the major decisions in your life to this point, only took a moment. The memories you look back on so fondly happened in a moment and will forever shape your story.

WHAT ARE THE MOMENTS YOU REMEMBER?
THINK ABOUT HOW THEY HAVE IMPACTED YOUR
STORY AND THE STORIES OF OTHERS.

- _____
- _____
- _____
- _____
- _____
- _____
- _____

As we seek to really live and embrace our stories, I pray we never forget the impact we can make in a moment. Jackie Robinson said so eloquently, "A life is not important except in the impact it has on other lives." Our own stories connect with other stories in countless ways. We will never know our impact on this side of eternity. It's a cheesy song, but Ray Boltz's song, "Thank You" paints a pretty cool picture of what will happen when we get to Heaven. He sings about the people we will meet in Heaven whom our stories have touched in some way. Some people we realize we impacted to the glory of God, while we had no idea that we helped change and shape the stories of others. When we give to the Lord, God uses us to help change the stories of others. Many of those we have impacted, we may not even remember. Living our millions of moments at an extraordinary level allows us to live our stories in such a manner to impact tens of thousands of lives.

I do not believe Abraham Lincoln envisioned his story and his moments tackling human rights, slavery, and the basic belief that God created all men and women to be equal, regardless of the color of their skin. I truly doubt that he believed he would have to wrestle with each of these issues in the middle of a civil war while trying to hold an entire nation together. What makes Abraham Lincoln stand out as one of the greatest presidents and leaders in the history of the United States was his ability to face these moments head-on and refuse to back down or shy away from these opportunities. I pray this quote, made by Lincoln in the midst of all these moments, may be an encouragement to you as you seek to live each moment fully.

What I cannot do, of course I will not do; but it may as well be understood, once for all, that I shall not surrender this game leaving any available card unplayed.

Refuse to walk away from your story without playing every card you have been given by your Creator. I cannot tell you which card you will need to play in each moment, but I know you will need to have them all available and ready. God does not give you a road map, but He continues to provide all you will need to continue to add to your story. The cards will vary and may cause you to dig deep to find them. Whenever I am facing a difficult situation or conversation, I always try to leave one "card" in my back pocket. It's a thought or idea I'm not willing to share up-front, but one I know I can use if I need it to accomplish the best. I don't always have to play it, but it is always there if I need it.

No one said it would be easy. It is worth it. It's worth everything. This is the story of your life. Take risks, throw caution to the wind, walk in faith, fight unfair, and never forget who goes before you and fights for you.

I love the thought of fighting unfair. God never fights fair. He is just and righteous, holy and perfect. I just don't believe "fair" is in His vocabulary. Our human understanding of "fair" is often so skewed. We always want things to be equal, the same, and equitable. God loves us too much to give everyone the exact same.

God has given you, and will always give you, what you need. You are unique and valued for just being you. God does not compare you with anyone else. This is why "fair," by human standards, is not utilized by God. God doesn't see everyone running the same race. He sees you running your race and living your story, and He is loving you and cheering you on.

I love reading the Israelite conquests in the Old Testament. They are never fair. The Egyptian army was massive, but so was the Red Sea (Exodus 14:28). The Promised Land, inhabited by hundreds of thousands of enemies, was simply handed over to Joshua and the Israelites, just as it was promised (Joshua 3-6). Gideon had his army reduced to three hundred men, went up against tens of thousands of enemy troops, and won with zero casualties (Judges 7:6-22). David and his mighty men took on hundreds, or thousands at a time, and returned victorious (II Samuel 23). God doesn't need things to be fair to write your story.

Jesus' parable of the lost sheep paints this perfect analogy (Luke 15:3-7). Jesus left everything to find one. Jesus left ninety-nine safely behind to pursue you. He left ninety-nine to find me. In today's world, many would argue this is far from "fair." The ninety-nine may have hurt feelings or believe they were not pursued with the same passion and provided the same attention. The truth is, at one time or another, you are going to need Jesus to find you in your story.

God will leave it all to find you and put you back in the middle of your story. Your story matters because God says it does. He proves it over and over again because He gives everything to find you. Jesus left the joy and perfection of Heaven to come to earth and die for you and for me. If this does not prove He is your biggest fan, I don't know what else could show you how much He loves you.

The best part of the story that often gets overlooked is how the Shepherd calls his friends and celebrates finding this one sheep. Jesus is our biggest fan and best cheerleader. He is thrilled when we live our stories in such a way that we are embracing our moments and living our God-given purposes and stories to the full! He doesn't gossip, scold, and shame us about why we got lost and off track in the first place. He just cares that we have been found.

I didn't really understand cheerleading growing up, and always thought it was sort of goofy. God has a great sense of humor. I never imagined I would be a "cheer-dad." Our daughter danced for a number of years growing up but was never interested in any kind of organized sports. During the summer before her seventh-grade year, she proudly announced she was trying out for the cheer squad. I was equal parts scared and shocked because I did not know how this was going to go. I truthfully did not think cheerleading was a part of her story. I was so wrong. She is a natural. She's already beautiful, like her momma. Thankfully, she inherited my outgoing approach and big mouth! Her personality shines through, and she's one amazing cheerleader.

So, guess what I do now? I go to the football games, and I don't watch the football! I don't sit with the football parents. I'm with the cheer moms! I look forward to timeouts and halftimes. I cheer on my cheerleader. It's awesome! Of course, I still passionately cheer for my son during soccer games, basketball games, and track meets, but this is different. I'm our daughter's biggest fan, and I now cheer for cheerleaders! (I discussed trying to get a "cheer-dad" shirt, hat, and matching socks, but it was not well received by our daughter.) This is a part of her story, and I am going to support it all the way. How much more does God cheer for and support us, since we are His children!

Believe God will be there, already ahead of you, and cheering for you. He's the One at the finish line of your story. When it hurts, when you stumble, and when you don't think you can just do it, He knows you can. He is the Voice in your soul and heart and mind, telling you your story is far from over. He is the One reminding you to throw off the weight, baggage, sins, and signs. The belief that you should be judged by so much more than your signs, that's Him too!

Paul talked about running this great race of faith (1 Corinthians 9:24-27). May we never forget that at the finish line is our Jesus, our God, and our final destination. He knows you can live this story because He created you to live it well. Wherever you are in your story, take the next step. Run this race with all you have to give. Embrace the next moment. Play the next card. Fight unfair.

Know that God meant it when He said you were special, precious, and His child. I pray my kids grow up to live their best story and change the world. I want them to help change the world right now because I know they have the gifts and the talents to do it. Imagine how God feels about you!

God desires to give you His best, which you will find when you seek Him with all your heart. Know He is always pursuing you. When you allow all the moments of your story to align in pursuit of Him, extraordinary always happens in your life. This is the extra to your ordinary. This is the key to your story. It's not magic, and it is not a twelve-step process. Leave the signs behind. Refuse to allow your life and your story to be defined by them. Realize God loves you for who you are and who you were created to be, not for the decisions you have made. Recognize that you have a story which is wonderful and so much bigger and better than your signs. Embrace this story and live every moment in the pursuit of the extraordinary. Let Jesus cheer you on and go before you to light the way. Jim Elliot said it best: "Wherever you are; be all there. Live to the hilt every situation you believe to be the will of God." Be present in every moment. They all matter because they all make up your extraordinary story.

God will always lead you and take you to a point to teach you something wonderful. After all, it is a race, and it is a journey. In order to live your story fully, sometimes, you must be willing to travel. You must be willing to keep running when you cannot see the finish line. Live one moment at a time, and live it to the full, with all that you have. Your story will stretch you because it's a big story waiting to be written and waiting to be lived. I don't know if I took the "road not taken," but I sure am glad I have taken the road God paved for me.

My mom loves to collect seashells, especially scallop shells. They come in all colors, shades, and sizes. She loves to find the ones that are "whole." These are the ones with no cracks, smooth edges, and the perfect circle shape at the top with the triangle edges at the bottom of each side. The triangle edges at the bottom sides of each scallop shell are called feet. It is extra special for my mom to find a shell free from any blemish with its two feet intact. I used to love collecting these shells for her when I would visit the beach.

Recently, my attitude towards these perfect shells has changed. I still like finding the ones with two perfect feet. What I look for in the top now has changed. I look for the scallop shells with rough edges. I like the ones with small cracks or a little piece missing out of the middle. I think the smooth ones with rough edges and a blemish or two are the best. They remind me of how we are designed to live our lives. We keep our feet intact and moving forward on the journey and keep embracing each moment of our stories. The cracks and rough edges, smooth parts and blemishes, simply mean that we have lived. It shows that we didn't stand on the sidelines and hide behind our signs. It shows we had faith in God to restore, renew, and create in us the passion to live our stories. They are not perfect, but they are oh so beautiful. I pray we see through our cracks, rough edges, and signs to embrace our stories.

Other people are waiting on your story as well. Others need those same cracks and holes and rough spots as encouragement to keep living their stories. They see the worn and blemished defects as a reminder that God is always in the restoration business and can use them in any way He chooses. People you know, strangers you have never met, those closest to you, and the ones with a singular encounter may all benefit from your moments lived well. While it is your story, may you never forget that your story intersects the stories of many others. God is orchestrating these stories together into the most beautiful masterpiece. He is piecing everyone together and making something beautiful and whole. Your story will impact people you have never met and will create ripple effects that, I pray, will be felt throughout eternity. You simply must be willing to live it.

I still wake up each day standing before my God with my sign, "NEED HELP". I pray you find yourself in the same place. The difference now is I hope you can lay this sign, and all your signs, at the feet of Jesus. I pray this frees you to live your story boldly. I believe in you and your story. God is the Author of every single story, and He is one amazing Author. I pray you embrace your story and never settle for anything less than the best. Embrace every day, every step, every page, every change, every chapter, every milestone and every moment. They are all a part of your story. No one else can live your story. Only you were created for these moments. These moments and your story are ready for extraordinary. A sign lasts for a moment. But a story, especially the great ones, lasts forever.

Expanded Scripture Guide

Chapter 1

Matthew 11:29-30 "Take my yoke upon you, and learn from me, for I am gentle and lowly in heart, and you will find rest for your souls. `For my yoke is easy, and my burden is light."

John 10:27 "My sheep hear my voice, and I know them, and they follow me."

John 15:12-17 "This is my commandment, that you love one another as I have loved you. `Greater love has no one than this, that someone lay down his life for his friends. `You are my friends if you do what I command you. `No longer do I call you servants, for the servant does not know what his master is doing; but I have called you friends, for all that I have heard from my Father I have made known to you. `You did not choose me, but I chose you and appointed you that you should go and bear fruit and that your fruit should abide, so that whatever you ask the Father in my name, he may give it to you. `These things I command you, so that you will love one another."

Chapter 3

Matthew 4:18-22 "While walking by the Sea of Galilee, he saw two brothers, Simon (who is called Peter) and Andrew his brother, casting a net into the sea, for they were fishermen. `And he said to them, 'Follow me, and I will make you fishers of men.' `Immediately they left their nets and followed him. `And going on from there he saw two other brothers, James the son of Zebedee and John his brother, in the boat with Zebedee their father, mending their nets, and he called them. `Immediately they left the boat and their father and followed him."

2 Corinthians 5:17 "Therefore, if anyone is in Christ, he is a new creation. The old has passed away; behold, the new has come."

Revelation 21:5 "And he who was seated on the throne said, 'Behold, I am making all things new.' Also he said, 'Write this down, for these words are trustworthy and true.'"

<u>Chapter 4</u>

Genesis 2:7-22 "Then the LORD God formed the man of dust from the ground and breathed into his nostrils the breath of life, and the man became a living creature. `And the LORD God planted a garden in Eden, in the east, and there he put the man whom he had formed. `And out of the ground the LORD God made to spring up every tree that is pleasant to the sight and good for food. The tree of life was in the midst of the garden, and the tree of the knowledge of good and evil.

A river flowed out of Eden to water the garden, and there it divided and became four rivers. `The name of the first is the Pishon. It is the one that flowed around the whole land of Havilah, where there is gold. `And the gold of that land is good; bdellium and onyx stone are there. `The name of the second river is the Gihon. It is the one that flowed around the whole land of Cush. `And the name of the third river is the Tigris, which flows east of Assyria. And the fourth river is the Euphrates.

The LORD God took the man and put him in the garden of Eden to work it and keep it. And the LORD God commanded the man, saying, 'You may surely eat of every tree of the garden, `but of the tree of the knowledge of good and evil you shall not eat, for in the day that you eat of it you shall surely die.'

Then the LORD God said, 'It is not good that the man should be alone; I will make him a helper fit for him.' Now out of the ground the LORD God had formed every beast of the field and every bird of the heavens and brought them to the man to see what he would call them. And whatever the man called every living creature, that was its name. `The man gave names to all livestock and to the birds of the heavens and to every beast of the field. But for Adam there was not found a helper fit for him. `So the LORD God caused a deep sleep to fall upon the man, and while he slept took one of his ribs and closed up its place with flesh. `And the rib that the LORD God had taken from the man he made into a woman and brought her to the man."

Matthew 7:1-5 "Judge not, that you be not judged. `For with the judgment you pronounce you will be judged, and with the measure you use it will be measured to you. `Why do you see the speck that is in your brother's eye, but do not notice the log that is in your own eye? Or how can you say to your brother, 'Let me take the speck out of your eye,' when there is the log in your own eye? `You hypocrite, first take the log out of your own eye, and then you will see clearly to take the speck out of your brother's eye."

2 Corinthians 1:3-4 "Blessed be the God and Father of our Lord Jesus Christ, the Father of mercies and God of all comfort, `who comforts us in all our affliction, so that we may be able to comfort those who are in any affliction, with the comfort with which we ourselves are comforted by God."

Job 40:1-7 "And the LORD said to Job:

'Shall a faultfinder contend with the Almighty?
`He who argues with God, let him answer it.'

Then Job answered the LORD and said:

'Behold, I am of small account; what shall I answer you?
`I lay my hand on my mouth.
I have spoken once, and I will not answer;
`twice, but I will proceed no further.'

Then the LORD answered Job out of the whirlwind and said:

'Dress for action like a man;
`I will question you, and you make it known to me.
Will you even put me in the wrong?
Will you condemn me that you may be in the right?
Have you an arm like God,
and can you thunder with a voice like his?'"

Job 42:1-6 "Then Job answered the LORD and said:

'I know that you can do all things,
`and that no purpose of yours can be thwarted.
"Who is this that hides counsel without knowledge?"
Therefore I have uttered what I did not understand,
`things too wonderful for me, which I did not know.
"Hear, and I will speak;
`I will question you, and you make it known to me."
I had heard of you by the hearing of the ear,
`but now my eye sees you;
therefore I despise myself,
`and repent in dust and ashes."

Chapter 5

1 John 4:18 "There is no fear in love, but perfect love casts out fear. For fear has to do with punishment, and whoever fears has not been perfected in love."

John 17:1-26 "When Jesus had spoken these words, he lifted up his eyes to heaven, and said, 'Father, the hour has come; glorify your Son that the Son may glorify you, since you have given him authority over all flesh, to give eternal life to all whom you have given him. And this is eternal life, that they know you, the only true God, and Jesus Christ whom you have sent. `I glorified you on earth, having accomplished the work that you gave me to do. `And now, Father, glorify me in your own presence with the glory that I had with you before the world existed.

`I have manifested your name to the people whom you gave me out of the world. Yours they were, and you gave them to me, and they have kept your word. `Now they know that everything that you have given me is from you. `For I have given them the words that you gave me, and they have received them and have come to know in truth that I came from you; and they have believed that you sent me. `I am praying for them. I am not praying for the world but for those whom you have given me, for they are yours. `All mine are yours, and yours are mine, and I am glorified in them. `And I am no longer in the world, but they are in the world, and I am coming to you. Holy Father, keep them in your name, which you have given me, that they may be one, even as we are one. `While I was with them, I kept them in your name, which you have given me. I have guarded them, and not one of them has been lost except the son of destruction, that the Scripture might be fulfilled. But now I am coming to you, and these things I speak in the world, that they may have my joy fulfilled in themselves. `I have given them your word, and the world has hated them because they are not of the world, just as I am not of the world. `I do not ask that you take them out of the world, but that you keep them from the evil one. `They are not of the world, just as I am not of the world. `Sanctify them in the truth; your word is truth. `As you sent me into the world, so I have sent them into the world. `And for their sake I consecrate myself, that they also may be sanctified in truth.

I do not ask for these only, but also for those who will believe in me through their word, that they may all be one, just as you, Father, are in me, and I in you, that they also may be in us, so that the world may believe that you have sent me. `The glory that you have given me I have given to them, that they may be one even as we are one, `I in them and you in me, that they may become perfectly one, so that the world may know that you sent me and loved them even as you loved me. `Father, I desire that they also, whom you have given me, may be with me where I am, to see my glory that you have given me because you loved me before the foundation of the world. `O righteous Father, even though the world does not know you, I know you, and these know that you have sent me. `I made known to them your name, and I will continue to make it known, that the love with which you have loved me may be in them, and I in them.'"

Chapter 6

Matthew 26:69-75 "Now Peter was sitting outside in the courtyard. And a servant girl came up to him and said, 'You also were with Jesus the Galilean.' `But he denied it before them all, saying, 'I do not know what you mean.' `And when he went out to the entrance, another servant girl saw him, and she said to the bystanders, 'This man was with Jesus of Nazareth.' `And again he denied it with an oath: 'I do not know the man.' `After a little while the bystanders came up and said to Peter, 'Certainly you too are one of them, for your accent betrays you.' `Then he began to invoke a curse on himself and to swear, 'I do not know the man' And immediately the rooster crowed. `And Peter remembered the saying of Jesus, 'Before the rooster crows, you will deny me three times.' And he went out and wept bitterly."

John 20:1-18 "Now on the first day of the week Mary Magdalene came to the tomb early, while it was still dark, and saw that the stone had been taken away from the tomb. `So she ran and went to Simon Peter and the other disciple, the one whom Jesus loved, and said to them, 'They have taken the Lord out of the tomb, and we do not know where they have laid him.'

So Peter went out with the other disciple, and they were going toward the tomb. `Both of them were running together, but the other disciple outran Peter and reached the tomb first. `And stooping to look in, he saw the linen cloths lying there, but he did not go in. `Then Simon Peter came, following him, and went into the tomb. He saw the linen cloths lying there, `and the face cloth, which had been on Jesus head, not lying with the linen cloths but folded up in a place by itself. `Then the other disciple, who had reached the tomb first, also went in, and he saw and believed; `for as yet they did not understand the Scripture, that he must rise from the dead. `Then the disciples went back to their homes.

`But Mary stood weeping outside the tomb, and as she wept she stooped to look into the tomb. `And she saw two angels in white, sitting where the body of Jesus had lain, one at the head and one at the feet. `They said to her, 'Woman, why are you weeping?' She said to them, 'They have taken away my Lord, and I do not know where they have laid him.' Having said this, she turned around and saw Jesus standing, but she did not know that it was Jesus. `Jesus said to her, 'Woman, why are you weeping? Whom are you seeking?' Supposing him to be the gardener, she said to him, 'Sir, if you have carried him away, tell me where you have laid him, and I will take him away.'

Jesus said to her, 'Mary.' She turned and said to him in Aramaic, 'Rabboni!' (which means Teacher). `Jesus said to her, 'Do not cling to me, for I have not yet ascended to the Father; but go to my brothers and say to them, "I am ascending to my Father and your Father, to my God and your God."' `Mary Magdalene went and announced to the disciples, 'I have seen the Lord'—and that he had said these things to her."

John 21:20-22 "Peter turned and saw the disciple whom Jesus loved following them, the one who also had leaned back against him during the supper and had said, 'Lord, who is it that is going to betray you?' `When Peter saw him, he said to Jesus, 'Lord, what about this man `Jesus said to him, 'If it is my will that he remain until I come, what is that to you? You follow me!'"

Chapter 7

I Samuel 16:6-13 "When they came, he looked on Eliab and thought, 'Surely the LORD's anointed is before him.' `But the LORD said to Samuel, 'Do not look on his appearance or on the height of his stature, because I have rejected him. For the LORD sees not as man sees: man looks on the outward appearance, but the LORD looks on the heart.'

Then Jesse called Abinadab and made him pass before Samuel. And he said, 'Neither has the LORD chosen this one.' `Then Jesse made Shammah pass by. And he said, 'Neither has the LORD chosen this one.' `And Jesse made seven of his sons pass before Samuel. And Samuel said to Jesse, 'The LORD has not chosen these.'

Then Samuel said to Jesse, 'Are all your sons here?' And he said, 'There remains yet the youngest, but behold, he is keeping the sheep.' And Samuel said to Jesse, 'Send and get him, for we will not sit down till he comes here.' `And he sent and brought him in. Now he was ruddy and had beautiful eyes and was handsome. And the LORD said, 'Arise, anoint him, for this is he.'`Then Samuel took the horn of oil and anointed him in the midst of his brothers. And the Spirit of the LORD rushed upon David from that day forward."

Proverbs 4:23 "Keep your heart with all vigilance, for from it flow the springs of life."

Chapter 8

Matthew 17:20 "He said to them, 'Because of your little faith. For truly, I say to you, if you have faith like a grain of mustard seed, you will say to this mountain, "Move from here to there," and it will move, and nothing will be impossible for you.'"

Romans 12:3 "For by the grace given to me I say to everyone among you not to think of himself more highly than he ought to think, but to think with sober judgment, each according to the measure of faith that God has assigned."

Hebrews 11:1 "Now faith is the assurance of things hoped for, the conviction of things not seen."

Matthew 4:7-10 "Jesus said to him, 'Again it is written, "You shall not put the Lord your God to the test."' `Again, the devil took him to a very high mountain and showed him all the kingdoms of the world and their glory. `And he said to him, 'All these I will give you, if you will fall down and worship me.' `Then Jesus said to him, 'Be gone, Satan!'"

Genesis 6:7-14 "So the LORD said, 'I will blot out man whom I have created from the face of the land, man and animals and creeping things and birds of the heavens, for I am sorry that I have made them.'

But Noah found favor in the eyes of the LORD. `These are the generations of Noah. Noah was a righteous man, blameless in his generation. Noah walked with God. `And Noah had three sons, Shem, Ham, and Japheth. `Now the earth was corrupt in God's sight, and the earth was filled with violence. `And God saw the earth, and behold, it was corrupt, for all flesh had corrupted their way on the earth. `And God said to Noah, 'I have determined to make an end of all flesh, for the earth is filled with violence through them. Behold, I will destroy them with the earth. `Make yourself an ark of gopher wood.'"

Genesis 2:5-6 "When no bush of the field was yet in the land and no small plant of the field had yet sprung up—for the LORD God had not caused it to rain on the land, and there was no man to work the ground, `and a mist was going up from the land and was watering the whole face of the ground."

I John 4:16 "So we have come to know and to believe the love that God has for us. God is love, and whoever abides in love abides in God, and God abides in him."

Matthew 22:37-40 "And he said to him, 'You shall love the Lord your God with all your heart and with all your soul and with all your mind. `This is the great and first commandment. `And a second is like it: You shall love your neighbor as yourself. `On these two commandments depend all the Law and the Prophets.'"

Chapter 9

Genesis 3:1-13 "Now the serpent was more crafty than any other beast of the field that the Lord God had made. He said to the woman, 'Did God actually say, "You shall not eat of any tree in the garden"?' `And the woman said to the serpent, 'We may eat of the fruit of the trees in the garden, `but God said, "You shall not eat of the fruit of the tree that is in the midst of the garden, neither shall you touch it, lest you die.'"

But the serpent said to the woman, 'You will not surely die. `For God knows that when you eat of it your eyes will be opened, and you will be like God, knowing good and evil.' `So when the woman saw that the tree was good for food, and that it was a delight to the eyes, and that the tree was to be desired to make one wise, she took of its fruit and ate, and she also gave some to her husband who was with her, and he ate.

Then the eyes of both were opened, and they knew that they were naked. And they sewed fig leaves together and made themselves loincloths.

And they heard the sound of the LORD God walking in the garden in the cool of the day, and the man and his wife hid themselves from the presence of the LORD God among the trees of the garden. `But the LORD God called to the man and said to him, 'Where are you?' `And he said, 'I heard the sound of you in the garden, and I was afraid, because I was naked, and I hid myself.' `He said, 'Who told you that you were naked? Have you eaten of the tree of which I commanded you not to eat?' `The man said, 'The woman whom you gave to be with me, she gave me fruit of the tree, and I ate.' `Then the LORD God said to the woman, 'What is this that you have done?' The woman said, 'The serpent deceived me, and I ate.'"

Joshua 24:1-15 "Joshua gathered all the tribes of Israel to Shechem and summoned the elders, the heads, the judges, and the officers of Israel. And they presented themselves before God. `And Joshua said to all the people, 'Thus says the LORD, the God of Israel, "Long ago, your fathers lived beyond the Euphrates, Terah, the father of Abraham and of Nahor; and they served other gods. `Then I took your father Abraham from beyond the River and led him through all the land of Canaan, and made his offspring many. I gave him Isaac. `And to Isaac I gave Jacob and Esau. And I gave Esau the hill country of Seir to possess, but Jacob and his children went down to Egypt. And I sent Moses and Aaron, and I plagued Egypt with what I did in the midst of it, and afterward I brought you out. `

Then I brought your fathers out of Egypt, and you came to the sea. And the Egyptians pursued your fathers with chariots and horsemen to the Red Sea. `And when they cried to the LORD, he put darkness between you and the Egyptians and made the sea come upon them and cover them; and your eyes saw what I did in Egypt. And you lived in the wilderness a long time.

Then I brought you to the land of the Amorites, who lived on the other side of the Jordan. They fought with you, and I gave them into your hand, and you took possession of their land, and I destroyed them before you. `Then Balak the son of Zippor, king of Moab, arose and fought against Israel. And he sent and invited Balaam the son of Beor to curse you, `but I would not listen to Balaam. Indeed, he blessed you. So I delivered you out of his hand. `And you went over the Jordan and came to Jericho, and the leaders of Jericho fought against you, and also the Amorites, the Perizzites, the Canaanites, the Hittites, the Girgashites, the Hivites, and the Jebusites. And I gave them into your hand. `And I sent the hornet before you, which drove them out before you, the two kings of the Amorites; it was not by your sword or by your bow. `I gave you a land on which you had not labored and cities that you had not built, and you dwell in them. You eat the fruit of vineyards and olive orchards that you did not plant."

'Now therefore fear the LORD and serve him in sincerity and in faithfulness. Put away the gods that your fathers served beyond the River and in Egypt, and serve the LORD. `And if it is evil in your eyes to serve the LORD, choose this day whom you will serve, whether the gods your fathers served in the region beyond the River, or the gods of the Amorites in whose land you dwell. But as for me and my house, we will serve the LORD.'"

Ephesians 2:10 (NIV) "For we are God's handiwork, created in Christ Jesus to do good works, which God prepared in advance for us to do."

Genesis 1:26-31 "Then God said, 'Let us make mankind in our image, in our likeness, so that they may rule over the fish in the sea and the birds in the sky, over the livestock and all the wild animals, and over all the creatures that move along the ground.'

So God created mankind in his own image,
in the image of God he created them;
male and female he created them.

God blessed them and said to them, 'Be fruitful and increase in number; fill the earth and subdue it. Rule over the fish in the sea and the birds in the sky and over every living creature that moves on the ground.'`Then God said, 'I give you every seed-bearing plant on the face of the whole earth and every tree that has fruit with seed in it. They will be yours for food. `And to all the beasts of the earth and all the birds in the sky and all the creatures that move along the ground—everything that has the breath of life in it—I give every green plant for food.' And it was so. `God saw all that he had made, and it was very good. And there was evening, and there was morning—the sixth day."

Exodus 13:21-22 "By day the LORD went ahead of them in a pillar of cloud to guide them on their way and by night in a pillar of fire to give them light, so that they could travel by day or night. `Neither the pillar of cloud by day nor the pillar of fire by night left its place in front of the people."

Numbers 13:26-30 "They came back to Moses and Aaron and the whole Israelite community at Kadesh in the Desert of Paran. There they reported to them and to the whole assembly and showed them the fruit of the land. `They gave Moses this account: 'We went into the land to which you sent us, and it does flow with milk and honey! Here is its fruit. `But the people who live there are powerful, and the cities are fortified and very large. We even saw descendants of Anak there. `The Amalekites live in the Negev; the Hittites, Jebusites and Amorites live in the hill country; and the Canaanites live near the sea and along the Jordan.'

Then Caleb silenced the people before Moses and said, 'We should go up and take possession of the land, for we can certainly do it.'"

Joshua 6:1-21 "Now Jericho was shut up inside and outside because of the people of Israel. None went out, and none came in. `And the LORD said to Joshua, 'See, I have given Jericho into your hand, with its king and mighty men of valor. `You shall march around the city, all the men of war going around the city once. Thus shall you do for six days. `Seven priests shall bear seven trumpets of rams' horns before the ark.

On the seventh day you shall march around the city seven times, and the priests shall blow the trumpets. `And when they make a long blast with the ram's horn, when you hear the sound of the trumpet, then all the people shall shout with a great shout, and the wall of the city will fall down flat, and the people shall go up, everyone straight before him.' `So Joshua the son of Nun called the priests and said to them, 'Take up the ark of the covenant and let seven priests bear seven trumpets of rams' horns before the ark of the LORD.' `And he said to the people, 'Go forward. March around the city and let the armed men pass on before the ark of the LORD.' `And just as Joshua had commanded the people, the seven priests bearing the seven trumpets of rams' horns before the LORD went forward, blowing the trumpets, with the ark of the covenant of the LORD following them. `The armed men were walking before the priests who were blowing the trumpets, and the rear guard was walking after the ark, while the trumpets blew continually.

But Joshua commanded the people, 'You shall not shout or make your voice heard, neither shall any word go out of your mouth, until the day I tell you to shout. Then you shall shout.' `So he caused the ark of the LORD to circle the city, going about it once. And they came into the camp and spent the night in the camp.

Then Joshua rose early in the morning, and the priests took up the ark of the LORD. `And the seven priests bearing the seven trumpets of rams' horns before the ark of the LORD walked on, and they blew the trumpets continually. And the armed men were walking before them, and the rear guard was walking after the ark of the LORD, while the trumpets blew continually. `And the second day they marched around the city once, and returned into the camp. So they did for six days.

On the seventh day they rose early, at the dawn of day, and marched around the city in the same manner seven times. It was only on that day that they marched around the city seven times. `And at the seventh time, when the priests had blown the trumpets, Joshua said to the people, 'Shout, for the LORD has given you the city. `And the city and all that is within it shall be devoted to the LORD for destruction. Only Rahab the prostitute and all who are with her in her house shall live, because she hid the messengers whom we sent.

But you, keep yourselves from the things devoted to destruction, lest when you have devoted them you take any of the devoted things and make the camp of Israel a thing for destruction and bring trouble upon it. `But all silver and gold, and every vessel of bronze and iron, are holy to the LORD; they shall go into the treasury of the LORD.'

So the people shouted, and the trumpets were blown. As soon as the people heard the sound of the trumpet, the people shouted a great shout, and the wall fell down flat, so that the people went up into the city, every man straight before him, and they captured the city. `Then they devoted all in the city to destruction, both men and women, young and old, oxen, sheep, and donkeys, with the edge of the sword."

Daniel 3:8-30 "Therefore at that time certain Chaldeans came forward and maliciously accused the Jews. `They declared to King Nebuchadnezzar, 'O king, live forever! `You, O king, have made a decree, that every man who hears the sound of the horn, pipe, lyre, trigon, harp, bagpipe, and every kind of music, shall fall down and worship the golden image. `And whoever does not fall down and worship shall be cast into a burning fiery furnace.

There are certain Jews whom you have appointed over the affairs of the province of Babylon: Shadrach, Meshach, and Abednego. These men, O king, pay no attention to you; they do not serve your gods or worship the golden image that you have set up.' `Then Nebuchadnezzar in furious rage commanded that Shadrach, Meshach, and Abednego be brought. So they brought these men before the king. `Nebuchadnezzar answered and said to them, 'Is it true, O Shadrach, Meshach, and Abednego, that you do not serve my gods or worship the golden image that I have set up? `Now if you are ready when you hear the sound of the horn, pipe, lyre, trigon, harp, bagpipe, and every kind of music, to fall down and worship the image that I have made, well and good. But if you do not worship, you shall immediately be cast into a burning fiery furnace. And who is the god who will deliver you out of my hands?'

Shadrach, Meshach, and Abednego answered and said to the king, 'O Nebuchadnezzar, we have no need to answer you in this matter. `If this be so, our God whom we serve is able to deliver us from the burning fiery furnace, and he will deliver us out of your hand, O king. `But if not, be it known to you, O king, that we will not serve your gods or worship the golden image that you have set up.'

Then Nebuchadnezzar was filled with fury, and the expression of his face was changed against Shadrach, Meshach, and Abednego. He ordered the furnace heated seven times more than it was usually heated. `And he ordered some of the mighty men of his army to bind Shadrach, Meshach, and Abednego, and to cast them into the burning fiery furnace. `Then these men were bound in their cloaks, their tunics, their hats, and their other garments, and they were thrown into the burning fiery furnace.

Because the king's order was urgent and the furnace overheated, the flame of the fire killed those men who took up Shadrach, Meshach, and Abednego. `And these three men, Shadrach, Meshach, and Abednego, fell bound into the burning fiery furnace.

Then King Nebuchadnezzar was astonished and rose up in haste. He declared to his counselors, 'Did we not cast three men bound into the fire?' They answered and said to the king, 'True, O king.' `He answered and said, 'But I see four men unbound, walking in the midst of the fire, and they are not hurt; and the appearance of the fourth is like a son of the gods.'

Then Nebuchadnezzar came near to the door of the burning fiery furnace; he declared, 'Shadrach, Meshach, and Abednego, servants of the Most High God, come out, and come here!' Then Shadrach, Meshach, and Abednego came out from the fire. `And the satraps, the prefects, the governors, and the king's counselors gathered together and saw that the fire had not had any power over the bodies of those men. The hair of their heads was not singed, their cloaks were not harmed, and no smell of fire had come upon them.

Nebuchadnezzar answered and said, 'Blessed be the God of Shadrach, Meshach, and Abednego, who has sent his angel and delivered his servants, who trusted in him, and set aside the king's command, and yielded up their bodies rather than serve and worship any god except their own God. `Therefore I make a decree: Any people, nation, or language that speaks anything against the God of Shadrach, Meshach, and Abednego shall be torn limb from limb, and their houses laid in ruins, for there is no other god who is able to rescue in this way.' `Then the king promoted Shadrach, Meshach, and Abednego in the province of Babylon."

Jonah 1:1-17 "Now the word of the LORD came to Jonah the son of Amittai, saying, 'Arise, go to Nineveh, that great city, and call out against it, for their evil has come up before me.' `But Jonah rose to flee to Tarshish from the presence of the LORD. He went down to Joppa and found a ship going to Tarshish. So he paid the fare and went down into it, to go with them to Tarshish, away from the presence of the LORD.

But the LORD hurled a great wind upon the sea, and there was a mighty tempest on the sea, so that the ship threatened to break up. `Then the mariners were afraid, and each cried out to his god. And they hurled the cargo that was in the ship into the sea to lighten it for them. But Jonah had gone down into the inner part of the ship and had lain down and was fast asleep. `So the captain came and said to him, 'What do you mean, you sleeper? Arise, call out to your god! Perhaps the god will give a thought to us, that we may not perish.'

And they said to one another, 'Come, let us cast lots, that we may know on whose account this evil has come upon us.' So they cast lots, and the lot fell on Jonah. `Then they said to him, 'Tell us on whose account this evil has come upon us. What is your occupation? And where do you come from? What is your country? And of what people are you?' `And he said to them, I am a Hebrew, and I fear the LORD, the God of heaven, who made the sea and the dry land.' `Then the men were exceedingly afraid and said to him, 'What is this that you have done!' For the men knew that he was fleeing from the presence of the LORD, because he had told them.

Then they said to him, 'What shall we do to you, that the sea may quiet down for us?' For the sea grew more and more tempestuous. `He said to them, 'Pick me up and hurl me into the sea; then the sea will quiet down for you, for I know it is because of me that this great tempest has come upon you.' `Nevertheless, the men rowed hard to get back to dry land, but they could not, for the sea grew more and more tempestuous against them. `Therefore they called out to the LORD, 'O LORD, let us not perish for this man's life, and lay not on us innocent blood, for you, O LORD, have done as it pleased you.' `So they picked up Jonah and hurled him into the sea, and the sea ceased from its raging. `Then the men feared the LORD exceedingly, and they offered a sacrifice to the LORD and made vows.

And the LORD appointed a great fish to swallow up Jonah. And Jonah was in the belly of the fish three days and three nights.

James 4:8 "Draw near to God, and he will draw near to you. Cleanse your hands, you sinners, and purify your hearts, you double-minded."

Romans 12:6 "Having gifts that differ according to the grace given to us, let us use them..."

Matthew 25:14-30 "For it will be like a man going on a journey, who called his servants and entrusted to them his property. To one he gave five talents, to another two, to another one, to each according to his ability. Then he went away. He who had received the five talents went at once and traded with them, and he made five talents more. So also he who had the two talents made two talents more. But he who had received the one talent went and dug in the ground and hid his master's money. Now after a long time the master of those servants came and settled accounts with them. And he who had received the five talents came forward, bringing five talents more, saying, 'Master, you delivered to me five talents; here, I have made five talents more.' His master said to him, 'Well done, good and faithful servant. You have been faithful over a little; I will set you over much. Enter into the joy of your master.' And he also who had the two talents came forward, saying, 'Master, you delivered to me two talents; here, I have made two talents more.' His master said to him, 'Well done, good and faithful servant. You have been faithful over a little; I will set you over much. Enter into the joy of your master.' He also who had received the one talent came forward, saying, 'Master, I knew you to be a hard man, reaping where you did not sow, and gathering where you scattered no seed, so I was afraid, and I went and hid your talent in the ground. Here, you have what is yours.' But his master answered him, 'You wicked and slothful servant! You knew that I reap where I have not sown and gather where I scattered no seed? Then you ought to have invested my money with the bankers, and at my coming I should have received what was my own with interest. So take the talent from him and give it to him who has the ten talents. For to everyone who has will more be given, and he will have an abundance. But from the one who has not, even what he has will be taken away. And cast the worthless servant into the outer darkness. In that place there will be weeping and gnashing of teeth.'

Chapter 10

1 Kings 18:20-40 "So Ahab sent to all the people of Israel and gathered the prophets together at Mount Carmel. And Elijah came near to all the people and said, 'How long will you go limping between two different opinions? If the LORD is God, follow him; but if Baal, then follow him.' And the people did not answer him a word.

Then Elijah said to the people, 'I, even I only, am left a prophet of the LORD, but Baal's prophets are 450 men. Let two bulls be given to us, and let them choose one bull for themselves and cut it in pieces and lay it on the wood, but put no fire to it. And I will prepare the other bull and lay it on the wood and put no fire to it. `And you call upon the name of your god, and I will call upon the name of the LORD, and the God who answers by fire, he is God.' And all the people answered, 'It is well spoken.'

Then Elijah said to the prophets of Baal, 'Choose for yourselves one bull and prepare it first, for you are many, and call upon the name of your god, but put no fire to it.' `And they took the bull that was given them, and they prepared it and called upon the name of Baal from morning until noon, saying, 'O Baal, answer us!' But there was no voice, and no one answered. And they limped around the altar that they had made. `And at noon Elijah mocked them, saying, 'Cry aloud, for he is a god. Either he is musing, or he is relieving himself, or he is on a journey, or perhaps he is asleep and must be awakened.' `And they cried aloud and cut themselves after their custom with swords and lances, until the blood gushed out upon them. `And as midday passed, they raved on until the time of the offering of the oblation, but there was no voice. No one answered; no one paid attention.

Then Elijah said to all the people, 'Come near to me.' And all the people came near to him. And he repaired the altar of the LORD that had been thrown down. `Elijah took twelve stones, according to the number of the tribes of the sons of Jacob, to whom the word of the LORD came, saying, 'Israel shall be your name,' `and with the stones he built an altar in the name of the LORD. And he made a trench about the altar, as great as would contain two seahs of seed. `And he put the wood in order and cut the bull in pieces and laid it on the wood. And he said, 'Fill four jars with water and pour it on the burnt offering and on the wood.' `And he said, 'Do it a second time.' And they did it a second time. And he said, 'Do it a third time.' And they did it a third time. `And the water ran around the altar and filled the trench also with water.

And at the time of the offering of the oblation, Elijah the prophet came near and said, 'O LORD, God of Abraham, Isaac, and Israel, let it be known this day that you are God in Israel, and that I am your servant, and that I have done all these things at your word. `Answer me, O LORD, answer me, that this people may know that you, O LORD, are God, and that you have turned their hearts back.'

Then the fire of the LORD fell and consumed the burnt offering and the wood and the stones and the dust, and licked up the water that was in the trench. `And when all the people saw it, they fell on their faces and said, 'The LORD, he is God; the LORD, he is God.' `And Elijah said to them, 'Seize the prophets of Baal; let not one of them escape.' And they seized them. And Elijah brought them down to the brook Kishon and slaughtered them there."

1 King 19:1-13 "Ahab told Jezebel all that Elijah had done, and how he had killed all the prophets with the sword. `Then Jezebel sent a messenger to Elijah, saying, 'So may the gods do to me and more also, if I do not make your life as the life of one of them by this time tomorrow.' `Then he was afraid, and he arose and ran for his life and came to Beersheba, which belongs to Judah, and left his servant there.

But he himself went a day's journey into the wilderness and came and sat down under a broom tree. And he asked that he might die, saying, 'It is enough; now, O LORD, take away my life, for I am no better than my fathers.' `And he lay down and slept under a broom tree. And behold, an angel touched him and said to him, 'Arise and eat.' `And he looked, and behold, there was at his head a cake baked on hot stones and a jar of water. And he ate and drank and lay down again. `And the angel of the LORD came again a second time and touched him and said, 'Arise and eat, for the journey is too great for you.' `And he arose and ate and drank, and went in the strength of that food forty days and forty nights to Horeb, the mount of God.

There he came to a cave and lodged in it. And behold, the word of the LORD came to him, and he said to him, 'What are you doing here, Elijah?' `He said, 'I have been very jealous for the LORD, the God of hosts. For the people of Israel have forsaken your covenant, thrown down your altars, and killed your prophets with the sword, and I, even I only, am left, and they seek my life, to take it away.'

And he said, 'Go out and stand on the mount before the LORD.' And behold, the LORD passed by, and a great and strong wind tore the mountains and broke in pieces the rocks before the LORD, but the LORD was not in the wind. And after the wind an earthquake, but the LORD was not in the earthquake. `And after the earthquake a fire, but the LORD was not in the fire. And after the fire the sound of a low whisper. `And when Elijah heard it, he wrapped his face in his cloak and went out and stood at the entrance of the cave. And behold, there came a voice to him and said, 'What are you doing here, Elijah?'

Chapter 11

John 5:1-9 "After this there was a feast of the Jews, and Jesus went up to Jerusalem. `Now there is in Jerusalem by the Sheep Gate a pool, in Aramaic called Bethesda, which has five roofed colonnades. `In these lay a multitude of invalids—blind, lame, and paralyzed. `One man was there who had been an invalid for thirty-eight years. `When Jesus saw him lying there and knew that he had already been there a long time, he said to him, 'Do you want to be healed?' `The sick man answered him, 'Sir, I have no one to put me into the pool when the water is stirred up, and while I am going another steps down before me.' `Jesus said to him, 'Get up, take up your bed, and walk.' `And at once the man was healed, and he took up his bed and walked."

Chapter 12

Mark 2:1-12 "And when he returned to Capernaum after some days, it was reported that he was at home. `And many were gathered together, so that there was no more room, not even at the door. And he was preaching the word to them. `And they came, bringing to him a paralytic carried by four men. `And when they could not get near him because of the crowd, they removed the roof above him, and when they had made an opening, they let down the bed on which the paralytic lay. `And when Jesus saw their faith, he said to the paralytic, 'Son, your sins are forgiven.' `Now some of the scribes were sitting there, questioning in their hearts, `'Why does this man speak like that? He is blaspheming! Who can forgive sins but God alone?' `And immediately Jesus, perceiving in his spirit that they thus questioned within themselves, said to them, 'Why do you question these things in your hearts? `Which is easier, to say to the paralytic, "Your sins are forgiven," or to say, "Rise, take up your bed and walk"? `But that you may know that the Son of Man has authority on earth to forgive sins'—he said to the paralytic— 'I say to you, rise, pick up your bed, and go home.' `And he rose and immediately picked up his bed and went out before them all, so that they were all amazed and glorified God, saying, 'We never saw anything like this!'

Chapter 13

John 11:1-44 "Now a certain man was ill, Lazarus of Bethany, the village of Mary and her sister Martha. `It was Mary who anointed the Lord with ointment and wiped his feet with her hair, whose brother Lazarus was ill. `So the sisters sent to him, saying, 'Lord, he whom you love is ill.' `But when Jesus heard it he said, 'This illness does not lead to death. It is for the glory of God, so that the Son of God may be glorified through it.'

Now Jesus loved Martha and her sister and Lazarus. `So, when he heard that Lazarus was ill, he stayed two days longer in the place where he was. `Then after this he said to the disciples, 'Let us go to Judea again.' `The disciples said to him, 'Rabbi, the Jews were just now seeking to stone you, and are you going there again?' `Jesus answered, 'Are there not twelve hours in the day? If anyone walks in the day, he does not stumble, because he sees the light of this world. `But if anyone walks in the night, he stumbles, because the light is not in him.' `After saying these things, he said to them, 'Our friend Lazarus has fallen asleep, but I go to awaken him.' `The disciples said to him, 'Lord, if he has fallen asleep, he will recover.' `Now Jesus had spoken of his death, but they thought that he meant taking rest in sleep. `Then Jesus told them plainly, 'Lazarus has died, `and for your sake I am glad that I was not there, so that you may believe. But let us go to him.' `So Thomas, called the Twin, said to his fellow disciples, 'Let us also go, that we may die with him.'

Now when Jesus came, he found that Lazarus had already been in the tomb four days. `Bethany was near Jerusalem, about two miles off,`and many of the Jews had come to Martha and Mary to console them concerning their brother. `So when Martha heard that Jesus was coming, she went and met him, but Mary remained seated in the house. `Martha said to Jesus, 'Lord, if you had been here, my brother would not have died. `But even now I know that whatever you ask from God, God will give you.' `Jesus said to her, 'Your brother will rise again.' `Martha said to him, 'I know that he will rise again in the resurrection on the last day.' `Jesus said to her, 'I am the resurrection and the life. Whoever believes in me, though he die, yet shall he live, `and everyone who lives and believes in me shall never die. Do you believe this?' `She said to him, 'Yes, Lord; I believe that you are the Christ, the Son of God, who is coming into the world.'

When she had said this, she went and called her sister Mary, saying in private, 'The Teacher is here and is calling for you.' `And when she heard it, she rose quickly and went to him. `Now Jesus had not yet come into the village, but was still in the place where Martha had met him. `When the Jews who were with her in the house, consoling her, saw Mary rise quickly and go out, they followed her, supposing that she was going to the tomb to weep there. `Now when Mary came to where Jesus was and saw him, she fell at his feet, saying to him, 'Lord, if you had been here, my brother would not have died.' `When Jesus saw her weeping, and the Jews who had come with her also weeping, he was deeply moved in his spirit and greatly troubled. `And he said, 'Where have you laid him?' They said to him, 'Lord, come and see.' `Jesus wept. `So the Jews said, 'See how he loved him!' `But some of them said, 'Could not he who opened the eyes of the blind man also have kept this man from dying?'

Then Jesus, deeply moved again, came to the tomb. It was a cave, and a stone lay against it. `Jesus said, 'Take away the stone.' Martha, the sister of the dead man, said to him, 'Lord, by this time there will be an odor, for he has been dead four days.' `Jesus said to her, 'Did I not tell you that if you be-lieved you would see the glory of God?' `So they took away the stone. And Jesus lifted up his eyes and said, 'Father, I thank you that you have heard me. `I knew that you always hear me, but I said this on account of the people standing around, that they may believe that you sent me.' `When he had said these things, he cried out with a loud voice, 'Lazarus, come out.' `The man who had died came out, his hands and feet bound with linen strips, and his face wrapped with a cloth. Jesus said to them, 'Unbind him, and let him go.'

Exodus 14:10-31 "When Pharaoh drew near, the people of Israel lifted up their eyes, and behold, the Egyptians were marching after them, and they feared greatly. And the people of Israel cried out to the Lord. `They said to Moses, 'Is it because there are no graves in Egypt that you have taken us away to die in the wilderness? What have you done to us in bringing us out of Egypt? `Is not this what we said to you in Egypt: "Leave us alone that we may serve the Egyptians"? For it would have been better for us to serve the Egyptians than to die in the wilderness.'

And Moses said to the people, 'Fear not, stand firm, and see the salvation of the LORD, which he will work for you today. For the Egyptians whom you see today, you shall never see again. The LORD will fight for you, and you have only to be silent.'

The LORD said to Moses, 'Why do you cry to me? Tell the people of Israel to go forward. `Lift up your staff, and stretch out your hand over the sea and divide it, that the people of Israel may go through the sea on dry ground. `And I will harden the hearts of the Egyptians so that they shall go in after them, and I will get glory over Pharaoh and all his host, his chariots, and his horsemen. `And the Egyptians shall know that I am the LORD, when I have gotten glory over Pharaoh, his chariots, and his horsemen.'

Then the angel of God who was going before the host of Israel moved and went behind them, and the pillar of cloud moved from before them and stood behind them, `coming between the host of Egypt and the host of Israel. And there was the cloud and the darkness. And it lit up the night without one coming near the other all night.

Then Moses stretched out his hand over the sea, and the LORD drove the sea back by a strong east wind all night and made the sea dry land, and the waters were divided. `And the people of Israel went into the midst of the sea on dry ground, the waters being a wall to them on their right hand and on their left. `The Egyptians pursued and went in after them into the midst of the sea, all Pharaoh's horses, his chariots, and his horsemen. `And in the morning watch the LORD in the pillar of fire and of cloud looked down on the Egyptian forces and threw the Egyptian forces into a panic, `clogging their chariot wheels so that they drove heavily. And the Egyptians said, 'Let us flee from before Israel, for the LORD fights for them against the Egyptians.'

Then the LORD said to Moses, 'Stretch out your hand over the sea, that the water may come back upon the Egyptians, upon their chariots, and upon their horsemen.' `So Moses stretched out his hand over the sea, and the sea returned to its normal course when the morning appeared. And as the Egyptians fled into it, the LORD threw the Egyptians into the midst of the sea. `The waters returned and covered the chariots and the horsemen; of all the host of Pharaoh that had followed them into the sea, not one of them remained. `But the people of Israel walked on dry ground through the sea, the waters being a wall to them on their right hand and on their left.

Thus the LORD saved Israel that day from the hand of the Egyptians, and Israel saw the Egyptians dead on the seashore. ˋIsrael saw the great power that the LORD used against the Egyptians, so the people feared the LORD, and they believed in the LORD and in his servant Moses."

Joshua 7:2-22 "The LORD said to Gideon, 'The people with you are too many for me to give the Midianites into their hand, lest Israel boast over me, saying, "My own hand has saved me." ˋNow therefore proclaim in the ears of the people, saying, "Whoever is fearful and trembling, let him return home and hurry away from Mount Gilead."' Then 22,000 of the people returned, and 10,000 remained.

And the LORD said to Gideon, 'The people are still too many. Take them down to the water, and I will test them for you there, and anyone of whom I say to you, "This one shall go with you," shall go with you, and anyone of whom I say to you, "This one shall not go with you," shall not go.'

So he brought the people down to the water. And the LORD said to Gideon, 'Every one who laps the water with his tongue, as a dog laps, you shall set by himself. Likewise, every one who kneels down to drink.' ˋAnd the number of those who lapped, putting their hands to their mouths, was 300 men, but all the rest of the people knelt down to drink water. ˋAnd the LORD said to Gideon, 'With the 300 men who lapped I will save you and give the Midianites into your hand, and let all the others go every man to his home.' ˋSo the people took provisions in their hands, and their trumpets. And he sent all the rest of Israel every man to his tent, but retained the 300 men. And the camp of Midian was below him in the valley.

That same night the LORD said to him, 'Arise, go down against the camp, for I have given it into your hand. ˋBut if you are afraid to go down, go down to the camp with Purah your servant. ˋAnd you shall hear what they say, and afterward your hands shall be strengthened to go down against the camp.' Then he went down with Purah his servant to the outposts of the armed men who were in the camp. ˋAnd the Midianites and the Amalekites and all the people of the East lay along the valley like locusts in abundance, and their camels were without number, as the sand that is on the seashore in abundance. ˋWhen Gideon came, behold, a man was telling a dream to his comrade. And he said, 'Behold, I dreamed a dream, and behold, a cake of barley bread tumbled into the camp of Midian and came to the tent and struck it so that it fell and turned it upside down, so that the tent lay flat.' ˋAnd his comrade answered, 'This is no other than the sword of Gideon the son of Joash, a man of Israel; God has given into his hand Midian and all the camp.'

As soon as Gideon heard the telling of the dream and its interpretation, he worshiped. And he returned to the camp of Israel and said, 'Arise, for the LORD has given the host of Midian into your hand.' ˋAnd he divided the 300 men into three companies and put trumpets into the hands of all of them and empty jars, with torches inside the jars. `And he said to them, 'Look at me, and do likewise. When I come to the outskirts of the camp, do as I do. `When I blow the trumpet, I and all who are with me, then blow the trumpets also on every side of all the camp and shout, "For the LORD and for Gideon."'

So Gideon and the hundred men who were with him came to the outskirts of the camp at the beginning of the middle watch, when they had just set the watch. And they blew the trumpets and smashed the jars that were in their hands. `Then the three companies blew the trumpets and broke the jars. They held in their left hands the torches, and in their right hands the trumpets to blow. And they cried out, 'A sword for the LORD and for Gideon!' Every man stood in his place around the camp, and all the army ran. They cried out and fled. `When they blew the 300 trumpets, the LORD set every man's sword against his comrade and against all the army. And the army fled as far as Beth-shittah toward Zererah, as far as the border of Abel-meholah, by Tabbath."

2 Samuel 23:8-39 "These are the names of the mighty men whom David had: Josheb-basshebeth a Tahchemonite; he was chief of the three. He wielded his spear against eight hundred whom he killed at one time.

And next to him among the three mighty men was Eleazar the son of Dodo, son of Ahohi. He was with David when they defied the Philistines who were gathered there for battle, and the men of Israel withdrew. `He rose and struck down the Philistines until his hand was weary, and his hand clung to the sword. And the LORD brought about a great victory that day, and the men returned after him only to strip the slain.

And next to him was Shammah, the son of Agee the Hararite. The Philistines gathered together at Lehi, where there was a plot of ground full of lentils, and the men fled from the Philistines. `But he took his stand in the midst of the plot and defended it and struck down the Philistines, and the LORD worked a great victory.

And three of the thirty chief men went down and came about harvest time to David at the cave of Adullam, when a band of Philistines was encamped in the Valley of Rephaim. `David was then in the stronghold, and the garrison of the Philistines was then at Bethlehem. `And David said longingly, 'Oh, that someone would give me water to drink from the well of Bethlehem that is by the gate!' `Then the three mighty men broke through the camp of the Philistines and drew water out of the well of Bethlehem that was by the gate and carried and brought it to David. But he would not drink of it. He poured it out to the LORD and said, 'Far be it from me, O LORD, that I should do this. Shall I drink the blood of the men who went at the risk of their lives?' Therefore he would not drink it. These things the three mighty men did.

Now Abishai, the brother of Joab, the son of Zeruiah, was chief of the thirty. And he wielded his spear against three hundred men and killed them and won a name beside the three. `He was the most renowned of the thirty and became their commander, but he did not attain to the three.

And Benaiah the son of Jehoiada was a valiant man of Kabzeel, a doer of great deeds. He struck down two ariels of Moab. He also went down and struck down a lion in a pit on a day when snow had fallen. `And he struck down an Egyptian, a handsome man. The Egyptian had a spear in his hand, but Benaiah went down to him with a staff and snatched the spear out of the Egyptian's hand and killed him with his own spear. `These things did Benaiah the son of Jehoiada, and won a name beside the three mighty men. `He was renowned among the thirty, but he did not attain to the three. And David set him over his bodyguard.

Asahel the brother of Joab was one of the thirty; Elhanan the son of Dodo of Bethlehem, `Shammah of Harod, Elika of Harod, `Helez the Paltite, Ira the son of Ikkesh of Tekoa, Abiezer of Anathoth, Mebunnai the Hushathite, `Zalmon the Ahohite, Maharai of Netophah, `Heleb the son of Baanah of Netophah, Ittai the son of Ribai of Gibeah of the people of Benjamin, `Benaiah of Pirathon, Hiddai of the brooks of Gaash, `Abi-albon the Arbathite, Azmaveth of Bahurim, Eliahba the Shaalbonite, the sons of Jashen, Jonathan, `Shammah the Hararite, Ahiam the son of Sharar the Hararite, `Eliphelet the son of Ahasbai of Maacah, Eliam the son of Ahithophel the Gilonite, Hezro of Carmel, Paarai the Arbite, Igal the son of Nathan of Zobah, Bani the Gadite, Zelek the Ammonite, Naharai of Beeroth, the armor-bearer of Joab the son of Zeruiah, Ira the Ithrite, Gareb the Ithrite, Uriah the Hittite: thirty-seven in all."

Luke 15:3-7 "So he told them this parable: `'What man of you, having a hundred sheep, if he has lost one of them, does not leave the ninety-nine in the open country, and go after the one that is lost, until he finds it? `And when he has found it, he lays it on his shoulders, rejoicing. `And when he comes home, he calls together his friends and his neighbors, saying to them, "Rejoice with me, for I have found my sheep that was lost." `Just so, I tell you, there will be more joy in heaven over one sinner who repents than over ninety-nine righteous persons who need no repentance.'

1 Corinthians 9:24-27 "Do you not know that in a race all the runners run, but only one receives the prize? So run that you may obtain it. Every athlete exercises self-control in all things. They do it to receive a perishable wreath, but we an imperishable. `So I do not run aimlessly; I do not box as one beating the air. `But I discipline my body and keep it under control, lest after preaching to others I myself should be disqualified."

For Further Study, Encouragement, & Accountability

There is no better way to connect with your story than through Scripture. Take time to read the Bible and let God speak to your heart, mind, and soul. The book of John is a great place to start, but you can read any book and Scripture, and I know God will guide you.

We all need encouragement and accountability as we live our stories. Take time to review this book, your answers, and the Scriptural passages with a friend, family member, or coworker.

Check out my blog (www.signtostory.org) for additional encouragement. If I can ever be an encouragement to you or pray for you specifically as you live your story, feel free to email at caswellcs@hotmail.com.

Know I have specifically prayed for you and everyone who would read this book. This has been a passion project that I knew I had to write. However God has used this book to remind you of all He wants to do in and through your life and story, I pray you always embrace your story and the great love of God. To God be the glory forever and ever. Amen.

ABOUT THE AUTHOR

Christopher David Smith is a passionate lover of life and tries to make the best of every moment God gives him. He believes in everyone's God-written story and that you should pursue your story and this life to the fullest with all you have in you. Jesus will take care of the rest.

Christopher has worked in the fields of youth, children, and family ministry. He loves teaching and leading, and currently serves as an elementary school principal. He feels his greatest accomplishments in life were convincing his beautiful bride to choose him, and having their two amazing teenage children. He and his family currently reside in North Carolina.

This is Christopher's first book, but he is an avid writer, and he would love for you to check out his blog, signtostory.org.

CPSIA information can be obtained
at www.ICGtesting.com
Printed in the USA
BVHW051627060521
606653BV00005B/458